PROUD PARENTHOOD

PROUD PARENTHOOD

JOSEPH L. FELIX

Abingdon   Nashville

Proud Parenthood

Copyright © 1977 by Abingdon

Library of Congress Cataloging in Publication Data

FELIX, JOSEPH L 1931–
    Proud parenthood.
    1. Parent and child. I. Title.
    BF723.P25F44   649.1′01′9   76-56256

ISBN 0-687-34540-5

MANUFACTURED BY THE PARTHENON PRESS AT
NASHVILLE, TENNESSEE, UNITED STATES OF AMERICA

PREFACE

It takes a while to write a good book. This one took forty-five years; I hope it has some merit.

I started writing the book in my high chair. One day Mother handed me a crayon and paper, and I discovered the thrill of expressing myself in writing. My feelings were primal, my thoughts rudimentary; and my written expression did almost nothing to communicate feelings or thoughts to anybody else.

But Mom has often marveled at how long I could sit and amuse myself this way. Of course, there was a lot happening with my mind and emotions besides the crude attempts at self-expression. I was busy learning. I learned a lot about what it was like to be a young human—oh, how many of those lessons have slipped away!

I learned joy, for example. The heart-lifting thrill of being swept up in Dad's strong hands and whisked through the air at a pace that left my stomach far behind. The refreshing comfort of splashing in a wading pool on a torrid summer afternoon. The tingling delight at seeing the look of pride on Mother's face with each of my "first" accomplishments.

I learned a bit of agony, too—getting scolded severely without understanding the reason, watching my popsicle melt on the sidewalk after falling off the stick, being trapped in my snowsuit when I had to use the bathroom and Mom was nowhere around.

There was so much to learn! No wonder the older "hoods" got to me before I was ready. Adulthood. Livelihood. Parenthood. Suddenly they were here—right here in my own life!

I kept writing. Along "Becoming Road" I must have told a few hundred people about the book I was going to publish someday. Where are they now? Will they read what I've written? Will they know that I've kept my word?

More important, will they know of my appreciation for what they contributed to my growth? The teachers who encouraged what must have been just a faint spark of literary talent? The students—classroom captives and counselees—who taught me more than I can ever return to them? God, let them know of my gratitude!

Thanks to Audrey, the girl up the street who typed my first "book" when I was ten or eleven.

Thanks to the guys I grew up with.

Thanks to Sandy, who came to a summer-school class and became my first counselee.

Thanks to a dozen encouraging secretaries, but especially to Donna, Joyce, and Lynn.

Thanks to hundreds of friends who contributed to this anthology of experiences.

Mostly, this book is my attempt to share things I've learned. Many of the friends who have taught me I've known only in books. I probably haven't come close to giving due credit for the ideas I've taken from some of them.

And then there were the many unrecognized authorities who have come to me as parents seeking help. How many valuable lessons for my own parenthood I've learned from them! In all, there are probably a few original ideas in this book, but I wouldn't be able to recognize them now.

Of my many debts of gratitude, none can compare with that I owe my family. The family of my birth gave me a solid spiritual foundation and room to grow. The family of my marriage gave me the fulfillment of proud parenthood. Thanks, my dearly beloved.

I'd like for you to know that my nine-year-old son is a writer, too. His lively imagination makes up for his occasional lapses in spelling. I've just finished reading his story about three boys who used to chase after dogs in the woods. One day what the boys thought was a dog turned out to be a rabid wolf. One of the boys, the story says, was bitten by the wolf, and "Dan got a very bad case of the rabbis."

Now, how can parenthood be anything but proud when you see talent like this? The moments of delight and exasperation, the experiences of hilarity that double you up with laughter, and the frustrations that push those "unmanly" tears through the ducts—these and all the other daily happenings bring me pride and gratitude.

In this book I try to share some of the things that have happened to me as a father of eight children and as a professional working with kids. I hope that what I have to say fits somewhere into your life.

CONTENTS

PROUD
PARENTHOOD

CHAPTER 1

OUR PRIDE AND JOY

LUCKY PARENTS

Parents are lucky to have children.

I say this fully aware that more than one father or mother is likely to have picked up this book in desperation. At this point such a parent may decide that the best thing to do with the book is to throw it at his kid.

In fact, it is precisely because I have felt the same way many times that I think it necessary to make such a statement. Surrounded by eight children of our own, Mrs. Felix and I have very often experienced the frustration that comes from having every known strategy fail. We know what it's like to apply all the psychology one has at one's disposal, only to find out that the child does as he pleases anyway.

But still, we recognize that we are very fortunate to have these eight individual, willful, unpredictable, fantastically wonderful children. Several couples we know have not been able to have children of their own. Their loneliness and their longing—the sorrow of their incompleteness—give us a deep appreciation of our sometimes alarming fertility.

Does this appreciation have something to do with the satisfaction I feel when I walk up to the clerk at McDonald's, put on my best poker face, and say, "Twenty-five hamburgers and ten fries, please"?

Well, even a psychologist has trouble analyzing his own behavior, but I think my hamburger order responds partly to a basic human need to strive for dramatic effect. It's the same motivation that influences your son when he looks in his lunch bag and shouts, "Oh, no, not bologna again!" on the day after his question, "Why don't you ever give us bologna on our sandwiches?" It's the drive that caused one young man to complain, "Why do you buy us TV dinners if you won't let us watch TV?" And it's the same motive that often prompts your children, in the summertime, when they've used up their original ideas for driving you crazy, to begin doing reruns.

Still, when the McDonald's clerk stares at me and I see his acned face wrinkle in an incredulous smile, I know that I derive much of my satisfaction from another kind of need. I realize that what I am feeling is *pride*. I'm proud of my family: incurably and unshamedly proud.

A SENSE OF ENDOWMENT

Then I recall the well-known truth from the book of Proverbs: "Pride goes before destruction." God-fearing(and God-loving) people have shrunk at this recollection. And rightfully so. Humility, we know, is truth. It recognizes that all the good in us comes from God, and that we are capable of nothing but evil on our own.

But we're not on our own.

The Father who created us and sent his Son to walk

beside us has given his Spirit to dwell in us. He has given us a share in the divine power of creation.

Pride now has a new meaning. It refers to the peaceful, wholesome, and refined feeling that comes from living well. It is a sense of endowment. We're proud of the wondrous gifts we have received, and we want to share our joy.

We have been allowed to share generously in the creation of human life. Each of our children reflects the image of his Creator, together with an assortment of characteristics inherited from his parents. Each child is flesh of my flesh, bone of my bone. And each child is flesh and bone of the beloved woman to whom I have given the flesh and bone that house my spirit.

This little boy who, quite oblivious of the time of year, hands me a homemade valentine in July, has his life because Mrs. Felix and I willed it. Free to choose whether to guard against conception and whether to snuff out the embryonic life, we allowed this Little Leaguer to come to bat and thrill us with his game-winning homer—this Scout to bring us the pride of his distinguished award.

And this boy—our firstborn—how did he come to be? How could parents so lacking in manual dexterity and construction skills fashion such a masterpiece—especially from the clumsy lovemaking that characterized our early marriage apprenticeship? "Can I hold my baby-sitter?" he asks, as we prepare him for his first evening without his parents or grandmother.

Here is a little girl who brightens a moment of extreme discouragement, a time when I am especially tired after a frustrating day. She leans over my chair, puts her head on my shoulder, and says from the heart, "Daddy, I love you so much."

And here is a son, our youngest, left at home after all the others have gone off to school. He has no neighborhood children to play with. But one day we find him sitting with a neighbor's dog, showing him the pictures in his book. Big Boy is a perfect audience. He never corrects or makes derogatory remarks.

Listen to children at play and share the charm of their dialogue:

"Let's say you're the nurse and I'm bringing my baby in because she's sick."

"What's the matter with your baby?"

"Well, I'm not too sure. She either has diabetes or diarrhea."

"Have you any parents?"

"Yes, two."

"Oh, I never rent to children with parents. They're too noisy and destructive."

"I'm going out to play ball with God."

"How can you play ball with God?"

"Easy. I just throw it up in the air, and God throws it back."

"I wonder what time it is."

"It must be after four."

"No, it can't be four o'clock yet, because my mother said I was to be home at four, and I'm not.

THE GIFT OF APPRECIATION

The charming things children say and do are effective reminders of what we would be missing if we had not been given the privilege of parenthood. But our appreciation increases when we realize that our children's sustained life is also a great blessing. Never do we treasure them more than when the possibility of losing them confronts us.

There was the little guy on the next block who was struck down by an auto. And the neighborhood boy who drowned in the swimming pool. These children were given to their parents for only a brief period of sharing and love. Then their Creator called them home—for reasons that cannot be understood within our narrow perspective.

Our three-year-old son was stricken with appendicitis. The doctor was concerned that the appendix might rupture. Infection had spread through the lad's body, and his fever was very high. One of the most haunting playbacks of our many meaningful experiences with our children is recalling the anxious hours we spent at his bedside. We remember him bathed in perspiration—sometimes semiconscious and barely able to recognize us, sometimes unconscious. We see his long, dark eyelashes lifting to show his huge brown eyes rolling. We hear him again as he calls—presumably to his older brother, as they play in his mind's eye—"Wait for me! Wait for me!"

"We can only be said to be alive," Thornton Wilder writes in *The Woman of Andros*, "in those moments when our hearts are conscious of our treasures." Every parent who has experienced the fear of having a child snatched away by death, and who has been spared this dreadful grief, has gained a deeper awareness of the treasure that children are.

Less anxious experiences can also increase our appreciation. It was one of those casual nights when the children were looking forward to a holiday from school on the next day. My wife and I had been out to a PTA meeting, and when we came home, several of the children were watching television. My wife joined them in front of the screen, and I retreated to my den. Somehow, the letdown after a busy day overcame several family members rather suddenly, and they fell asleep in scattered areas of the house.

When I came from the den, I found my wife and several

of the children asleep in the living room. I looked in on the others who had already found their way to bed, and I was about to wake up the living room sleepers so they could turn in when I realized that we were one child short!

Panic struck.

First, I looked in the usual places one might expect to find a sleeping child. Then I checked some of the more unusual places. No sleeping child. I wondered whether he might have stepped outside briefly or could be playing an unofficial game of hide-and-seek.

After several minutes of searching, I began to have some horrendous thoughts. I imagined him slumped in some corner of the house (the doctor, after all, had indicated a mild heart murmur in infancy). I imagined him drowned in the bathtub. I imagined him kidnapped by someone who had entered and exited in some undetected manner.

Reluctantly I awakened my wife, and she joined me in the search. Our interaction compounded the worry. Then our oldest children joined us also. It seemed an endless time of searching. My wife began to cry.

Then from the other room, our oldest son announced, "I found him!"

The little guy was curled up in his wardrobe. He had made his bed ready in a very sleepy condition and had evidently mistaken the bottom of the wardrobe for the bed. When we questioned him about it the next morning, he had no idea what had happened.

The strange mixture of intense emotions that one feels at a time such as this is indescribable. I wanted to be angry but could not. I wanted to cry but dared not. More than anything else, I suppose, I felt a deep sense of appreciation for this wonderful gift of a son. I knew at that time, as never before, how precious he was to me and how rich I was to have him.

A father felt tremendous love for his son that evening. But the son had no awareness of this emotion. He was asleep and obviously knew nothing of the closeness I felt at that hour of the night. And yet my life was enriched as I embraced and cherished him.

THE ENRICHMENT OF GIVING

This was perhaps the clearest insight I have ever had into that paradoxical law that pervades our lives and insures that we do indeed receive as we give. The functioning of the great law is most obvious when we share nonmaterial things. If two men pool their financial resources, one can use only what the other does not. But let two men share ideas, and each has use of the total idea bank. Love, although often dependent on material things for expression, transcends the limits of the material. Whenever we give it, we ourselves are enriched.

This, in fact, is the reason above all others that parents are lucky to have children. They provide us with a constant opportunity for personal growth toward self-fulfillment. They furnish a unique and inescapable demand for giving of ourselves.

From the day Mrs. Felix and I stopped waiting for the menstrual flow and began planning for the future of a newly created life, each child has helped us grow as persons. Throughout the months of pregnancy, with all its awkwardness and discomfort, we have lived in anticipation and stored up love to bestow on our new offspring—another mouth to feed, another body to clothe, another mind to educate. With every plan, with every hope, with every expectation, another bit of love has sprouted in our hearts.

I'm talking like a proud father. I take pleasure in my children and in the opportunity for self-giving they have brought me.

This kind of pride is very different from the intellectual pride referred to in Proverbs. The false pride that goes before destruction is a conviction of one's own self-sufficiency. It is a distorted belief that closes us off from others and builds a defense against seeking the truth about ourselves and our actions. One who is proud in this sense is apt to plunder the personalities around him rather than seek to share what has been received.

In contrast, the pride of parenthood is a generous pride. It is based on gratitude for the opportunities for personal development that come with being a mother or father.

Every father who provides well for his family has abundant reasons for pride. Half a century ago children could be an economic asset, but today they add to the family's financial burden from birth through college. To the breadwinner, this often means working longer hours than the human body and mind seem able to tolerate.

Spiritual needs also require attention. A good father spends the time and energy necessary to care for the souls of his children. He is devoted to the whole person of each of his offspring. This devotion requires self-sacrifice: setting personal interests aside to immerse oneself in the world of the child, tolerating the squabbling that inevitably results from sibling rivalry, resisting the compulsion to gain both escape and physical rest in the reclining chair. Each of these acts of giving makes a father richer.

But in the exchequer of self-giving, a mother's love makes the wealth of even the most devoted father look like penury. Almost inevitably—even in this era of liberated womanhood—children are identified most closely with their mothers. From infancy, the physical and spiritual contact between a child and his mother is extensive and intensive. Thus, a mother's giving exerts an immeasurably powerful influence on the child's development.

Innumerable are the forms of a mother's self-giving. Lovingly, she accepts the pains of child bearing. Selflessly, she exerts the energy and invests the time it takes to care for her home and family. Untiringly, she sits at the bedside of her sick child. Willingly, she gives up comforts and luxury to help provide for her child's education. And with every gift of herself she is enriched. Mothers have much to be proud of.

The pride of parenthood is good. It brings confidence in our ability to deal with the countless challenges that go along with our state in life. It enables us to lift our heads a little higher at a time when many outside influences are working to destroy our sense of dignity.

OUTMODED ATTITUDES

Take, for instance, the changing outlook on procreation. There was a time when attitudes toward human sexuality were so puritan that a pregnant woman was ashamed to be seen in public.

The expectant mother used to get disapproving looks from many of the proper people around her. "We know what you've been doing!" they seemed to say. To wear a maternity dress was to confess to all the world that one had engaged in an animalistic act.

Over the years people's attitudes toward sex began to mellow somewhat, and something of the beauty of human reproduction began to be emphasized. Still, there were many who frowned upon parents who chose to have large families.

And then there were the jokers. "Do you have any other hobbies?" was one kind of biting remark directed at the parent with several children. Lacking evidence to the contrary, these parents were always assumed to be either faithful Catholics or oversexed Protestants.

CURRENT ATTITUDES

We've come a long way in our attitudes toward human sexual functions. Intercourse is now quite mod. It's a considerably more comfortable situation for the average husband and wife—except that now some people can't understand why you limit the sharing of this experience to a single partner. If the impressions created by the mass media are accurate, the everyday housewife who used to invite the mailman in for a cup of coffee on an especially cold morning is now sharing much more intimately. And tomorrow the milkman comes.

This may be some people's idea of progress, but it hasn't much improved the position of those parents who opt to have large families. For today we have an organization called Zero Population Growth. It wouldn't surprise me to learn that a manufacturer had come out with a cigar wrapped in paper that read, "Pardon us for adding to the world's problems."

Modern attitudes toward large families make you feel like jumping in the ocean and pulling a wave over you if you dare have more than one child. Legislation has been proposed that would impose hardships on parents who choose to fill their homes with the tears and laughter of offspring. This is reminiscent of a headline the *Boston Herald* carried on a report of an auto accident: "Father of Eleven Fined for Not Stopping."

One can easily imagine a federal agent whose job it is to check out every woman with a protruding abdomen. The agent gives the expectant mother a suspicious look, and if she's lucky enough for this to be her first child, she holds up one finger. Two fingers mean this is the second child, and so forth. But woe to that mother who needs more than one hand!

IMPORTANCE OF FREEDOM

I do not mean to make light of a problem as serious as overpopulation. The starvation of countless human beings is a tragedy that defies description. I have also seen projections that suggest that the situation could get worse.

Statistics, though, are notorious for the ease with which they can be misused. It seems like a classic case of lying with statistics to move from the serious dimensions of overpopulation in the undeveloped countries of our world to the conclusion that family size must be restricted in our generally affluent society.

I can readily respect the decision of parents who see it as their responsibility to limit family size. Freedom to follow their consciences is critically important. On the other hand, it is just as important that parents who choose to make the sacrifices necessary to have a large family have their freedom preserved. The thought of federal legislation that would restrict family size is horrifying. The humiliation that comes from the attitudes of many "modern thinkers" is almost as disturbing.

I think it's time to reverse the trend. One of life's proudest moments should be the telephone call to the in-laws to inform them of their new grandchild. And cigars should always be passed out with enthusiasm.

Every parent who cooperates in bringing a child into the world and helps that child get ready for life has countless reasons to be proud. Each problem parents face with some measure of success—however limited—contributes to the formation of both parent and child.

ABUNDANT LIVING

Parenthood packs a rich abundance of living into a few wonderfully hectic years. In the loving intimacy of sexual intercourse, a couple blend their miraculous human endowments and generate new life. With the short span of about twenty years, they nurture this life from a condition of complete parental dependency to the physical, emotional, and intellectual maturity that enables their offspring to go out on his own into the adult world.

And oh, the dreams and hopes, the joys and expectations, the crises and sorrows, that are crowded into this short time! A mother holds her infant to her breast, and her entire body pulsates with delight in the being she has brought into the world and now sustains with nourishment. A father lifts his infant son to look straightforward into his wide-open, expectant eyes. The tiny, toothless laugh that comes back to him seems to say, "Thanks for being my daddy." Thus parents delight as they share in the divine power of creation.

Then, almost as imperceptibly as one motion-picture scene unfolds into another, the infant whom Mother embraces and Father looks proudly upon grows into a school-age child, a searching adolescent, an independent adult. Picture the preschool young lady, the image of motherhood, as she drags her doll by the foot. The first-grader who lassoes your heart as he eases ever so unsurely out the door to start a new phase of his life. The growing boy who always seems to know just how much soap and water to use so that most of the dirt will come off on the towel. The excited son and daughter moving all too hurriedly past that perfect age when they're too old to cry at night and too young to borrow the car. The teen-age girl with her twelve-year-old clothes, six-year-old talk, and twenty-year-old sophistication.

And then, suddenly, she's really eighteen—and she and her childhood friends are off to college.

Through college the children dance in a whirlwind, and soon there comes that last June, when all the graduates leave college to look for positions and wind up getting jobs.

Once again your darling daughter is off—this time with the guy who has stolen her heart. Things are quiet again in the house; there's an overwhelming emptiness in your heart; and the exciting drama of parenthood has reached its denouement.

You feel spent then, and rightfully so. Raising a family is an exhausting task.

Through it all we have constant reminders of how hectic our lives are. A few days before Christmas one mother was making some last-minute purchases. She stood next to the harried clerk, who was obviously overwhelmed by the rush, as she filled out the sales slip. The customer gave her name and address. The clerk, looking around at the swarm of shoppers, commented, "It's really a madhouse, isn't it?"

The mother looked dismayed. "No," she replied in well-frozen words, "it's a private residence."

THE DIGNITY OF PARENTHOOD

Much of my reverence for fatherhood came from my own Dad. This excellent man lived and died a father in every good sense of the word. I know I was in his thoughts and in his prayers that morning a few weeks back when he told Mom he was just too weak to go on and lay down peacefully to die. I know I was in his prayers and thought *every* day and that he continues even now to be with me and help me. But I am just beginning to know how vital his example and support have been to my own success as a father. In countless ways, Dad taught me the value of human life, the dignity of parenthood, and the beauty of the father-son relationship.

Hopefully, I have passed on some of these invaluable lessons to my children. Hopefully, too, my children sense the awe that comes to me each time I reawaken to the wonder of fatherhood. Kings and prophets have gone to their graves without experiencing the wonder I have known.

Symphonic music is beautiful to hear, but in the realm of delightful sounds it plays second fiddle to the laughter—even the howls—of children. The story is told that in the California gold-rush days a lady took her baby to the theater one evening. Just as the orchestra began to play, the child started to cry.

"Stop those fiddles and let the baby cry," called a man in the pit. "I haven't heard such a sound in ten years!" Wild applause greeted his request. The orchestra stopped playing, and the baby continued its performance with great enthusiasm.

Bringing children into the world does much more than just insure the preservation of the race. Children enlarge our hearts. They bring out in us the most noble of aspirations and generous affection. They brighten the firesides of our lives with their innocent smiles.

CHAPTER 2

PARENT AS YOU ARE

LUCKY CHILDREN

Children are lucky to have parents, too. Ask any orphan.

In every parent's life there are many times when we find ourselves wondering whether our children wouldn't be better off without us. We see the many fears and inhibitions they develop, and we recognize contributing causes in our own behavior. We look back on the many times our words or actions have clearly not been in the best interests of our children. Deluged with regret, we feel certain that the harmful effects of our mistakes have far exceeded any benefits our offspring might have derived from having us around.

It's true of every parent that some of our acts have a harmful effect on our children. Out of the mouths of babes, for instance, come words we should never have uttered. But as the little guy said when he slipped trying to get the cookies, knocked the jar of honey off the shelf, broke four of Mom's good dinner plates, and spilled the honey over the new all-weather, now all gooey carpet, "Heck, nobody's perfect."

Even with all this, our children are richer for having us as parents. We'll look at why this is true in a moment. Right now I want to emphasize that this applies to you—just as you are now. Your natural parenting self is enriching to your child.

As you go through your years in never-never land (never enough time, never enough money, never enough sleep), just be sure there's always enough love. Most young people who have been deprived of the loving care of a mother and father crave the attention that only a parent could give. They long for the generous love, the protection and essentials of life, provided by a dedicated father, a dedicated mother.

Our world is full of orphans: the young of many species are given life and then abandoned. When the young amoeba breaks off from the parent cell, it has no knowledge of the wonder of the parent-child relationship. Absent is the intimate, vital bond between the body of the mother and the body of the young offspring. Missing, too, is the love of a father who takes pride in providing for the material needs of this new life. The same is true of the crab, who springs from eggs pushed into the water and abandoned.

Almost certainly, if the test-tube baby ever becomes real, he will be less complete for not having known the comfort of a mother's womb. He is sure to have a strong yearning for the protection of a real parent. Never will the test-tube baby know what it's like to be sheltered for nine months in the embrace of maternity, where every heartbeat transmits a message of love.

But the benefit the child derives from parental love and care is only one reason children are lucky to have parents. There are many others. Parents provide models for children, giving them a concept of what it means to be a human being. Through our mistakes and through our teaching, children learn many lessons of life. The examples we give provide a framework of beliefs and values that has a dramatic influence on the kind of people they become.

Above all else, however, our children benefit from our *giving*. To the infant, the parent gives the loving protection of nurturing and caring for every need. In childhood, there is the provision of food, clothing, shelter, and a host of other material, psychological, and spiritual needs. Finally, as the child progresses through adolescence and reaches maturity, the parent gives the greatest gift of all: the independence that permits the young adult to choose, on his own, to give the same kind of love he has learned from his parents.

LEARNING TO LOVE

Here, then, is the chief reason children are lucky to have parents. By experiencing the love their parents give them, they themselves learn to love. And as they grow under the protective mantle of parental care, they eventually reach a point where they can make a series of decisions to give of themselves and practice the life of love they have learned from their parents.

As our oldest children reach maturity, a wave of mixed emotion floods my being. I ache with the realization that they have come of age—so near the beginning of our acquaintance—just as we had begun to stroll together through the gardens of our souls. And yet I rejoice at their attainment of the ability to move forward in the life-style they choose. It's been said that one good thing about the generation gap is that our kids do eventually find themselves on our side of it.

One reason the child must experience receiving love in order to learn to give it is that loving is contrary to many of the basic drives of our nature. We are inclined to insure our own survival—indeed, our own comfort—first and foremost. Unless we have the security of having our own needs met, we are not likely to turn outside ourselves for the purpose of giving to others.

Thus the child who has never experienced parental love is often left with a primary need unmet. Throughout his life he is apt to be more concerned with his own rights and the fulfillment of his own needs than with what he can give to others. Conversely, it is the child who has had the richest supply of love, with proper attention to his spiritual, physical, and psychological needs, who is in best position to be generous toward others. By loving the child, we teach how to love.

We looked at some of the forms of these love lessons in the first chapter. The relationship between parent and child includes countless instances of self-giving.

Opportunities to teach love through self-giving are not, of course, limited to parent-child relationships. From the parent's viewpoint, we are surrounded by situations that cry out for a part of ourselves. We need to look only a short distance to find a suffering person in need of solace, a hungry person to feed, a thirsty person to give drink. Unfortunately, though, unless someone confronts us with an appeal for help, we can often go for long periods of time without extending a helping hand.

Then, too, most institutional appeals tend to be somewhat impersonal, and frequently our contributions are more mechanical than genuine. If we rely exclusively on this kind of giving, love becomes more and more abstract—a general quality we think we possess but do not apply in any immediate, active way.

To fall into this trap with children around is virtually impossible. Just by being present, children make a constant demand for parent self-giving. Parental love cannot be a generalized, abstract matter. It is, in fact, *very* specific, always a matter of the here and now.

THE PURGATION OF LOVE

A more real problem for the average parent is that there is far too much here and now. Unable to get far enough away from everyday concerns to maintain perspective, mothers and fathers often exaggerate the importance of the ordinary difficulties of family life. Minor frustrations take a heavier toll than they should, hampering the ability for spontaneous self-giving.

And so our love encounters difficulty. We explode over some event that we later see clearly as inconsequential; at the time it just happens to be number 1001 for our 1000-capacity Frustration Endurance System. But this, too, will pass. The cloud from our explosion will dissipate; we'll do our best to repair damages; and we'll get on with the business of loving.

The difficulties merely serve to purify love. So it is, too, when our love seems to go unreturned and unappreciated. Love that is without such obstacles soon decays into mere selfishness. We come to cherish a loved one because of what that person does for us—fulfilling our dependency needs, returning our love, giving us a good feeling that we have done something worthwhile.

When we love without hope of return, our love takes on a new character. We put aside our own needs and concern ourselves entirely with giving. Love is then most ennobling, most enriching, most sustaining.

This brings us to a new perspective. In discussing the blessings of parenthood in chapter 1, we looked principally at the aspects that tend to evoke positive emotions—the charm that children add to our lives and the opportunity they bring for personal growth through love. Now we are seeing more clearly that some of parenthood's richest blessings are well disguised. Problems that make loving more difficult also increase the self-enrichment we derive from that love. So also the love lessons we teach take on additional value because of the child's urgent need.

Ironically, in those situations where love is most needed, loving is usually most difficult. The person who would benefit most from our love is typically least lovable. When a child refuses to obey or directs a biting insult at us, it is difficult to recognize the need for love that underlies this behavior. It requires genuine self-immolation to be acceptant, understanding, and loving at such a time.

In this imperfect world, our children will inevitably express their needs in imperfect ways. When we succeed in looking beyond their offensive words and actions, recognizing their need for love, and giving of ourselves despite our feelings, we are doubly enriched. And we teach a powerful lesson in love.

In situations of greatest need, the beneficial effects of our self-giving will often be hidden for a long time. But there is always reason for optimism. Even when our children seem to reject all that we would give them to make their future lives happier, we can continue to hope. Perhaps somewhere in the souls of our children—after all the insecurities and psychological hang-ups are stripped away and all the pains and agonies are survived—a spark of love that we have planted will burst into flame.

DEVELOPING A STYLE

I have a deep conviction that the children God has given us are exactly the children we need to become our best possible selves. Humanly weak as we are, we may fall short of that ideal; but the potential is definitely there.

From all eternity God knew that we would all make many mistakes in raising our kids. And yet he trusted us with the awesome responsibility of bringing life into the world. With his continuing guidance, even our failures will be converted to good use in helping our children.

It sometimes seems to me that I have the perfect natural temperament to be the world's worst father. As a hermit I might be a singular success. But this is the me to whom God has handed the priceless treasure of parenthood. As I try to do my best with it, I rely on his support and guidance.

My style of parenting will be different from yours. You need to develop a style of your own—one that builds on your personal strengths and takes account of your unique needs. Within the resources you bring to parenthood you will find means enough to deal with the diverse challenges and problems that present themselves. You can make your parenthood the rich, fulfilling experience God intends it to be.

It is only in giving ourselves totally to the fullness of our state of life that we can really find joy. And we do need to find joy if we are to be fully alive and share our love with our spouse and children. Joy is essential in order that the mistakes we make, the annoyances and inconveniences we encounter daily, will not seriously harm us or stand in the way of moving forward to a happier life.

I want this book to add joy to your parenting. If it doesn't, throw it out. In the chapters ahead I'll suggest some ideas that I've found helpful. Some of these may fit well into your unique style of parenthood. I strongly encourage you to capitalize on whatever strategies do seem to fit. Just as forcefully, though, I would steer you clear of any feelings of guilt or regret if certain other ideas are impractical for you.

Choose and use those that are helpful. They will lead you to a greater satisfaction and pride in your role as a parent. If you feel better about your parenthood, the quality of your performance will also increase. You may not see the change—any more than you can see your children growing. But you'll be developing into the kind of parent you want to be.

Let parenthood be a creative growth experience for you, not a burdensome duty. Recognize that growth seldom occurs in a straight line. Almost always, genuine growth comes in spirals. Starting in the present, we move ahead a little, gain new knowledge or understanding, then circle around, slip back, consider what has happened, and integrate the new with the old. The past and the future are constantly acting on each other.

No parent devotes all of his or her resources to rearing the children. Part of our inner resources must remain available for our own continuing development as adults. We all need to set goals for today's beginning, taking account of our own psychological needs as well as those of our children. If we decide to work to change our own behavior, we must first be certain that those needs of ours that we sacrifice have other means of realization.

THE STRUGGLE FOR FREEDOM

Viewed in this perspective, parenthood is a challenging struggle for freedom. In chapter 1 we talked about the need to struggle against outside forces that would restrict our freedom. Along with other groups that have had to exert systematic effort to attain freedom, parents must struggle against the attitudes that threaten them with oppression and seek to rob them of their human dignity.

But there is another kind of struggle that is often even more difficult. If we are to be proud of our parenthood, we must fully open ourselves to this pride. We must learn to delight in our successes. At the same time, we must continually fight against psychological needs and personal traits that hinder our attainment of the goals we set. The struggle to be the kind of parents we want to be is never-ending, for we are essentially struggling for freedom from our own selves.

As we struggle, we grow. Recognizing this growth can help us deal with the new demands of each day. Our personalities are constantly changing; they do not stop suddenly at the end of adolescence and remain permanently fixed. We change as we live through critical life experiences, interacting with various people in our environment. We learn to maintain equilibrium by adapting to the pressures we feel from various directions at different times. Each new stage of life demands—and gets—an added degree of personal growth. We progress toward freedom.

Clearly, psychology has much to contribute in our struggle for freedom. It has helped many parents move forward to a happier, more effective kind of life. But we do need to keep an eye on the positive side of parenthood. We need to let our knowledge of psychology help us have the wholesome, satisfying life-style that God intends families to have.

It is important to realize that the very fight for freedom is fulfilling. As we apply ourselves to the sincere effort of becoming better parents, we find in the struggle the realization of our potential. We come to view ourselves with increasing acceptance, to see ourselves as dynamic, becoming human beings. The nature of our human existence is a continuous evolution toward the quality of living we seek.

THE PROBLEM OF GUILT

To help you toward the kind of freedom that will increase your pride in parenthood is an important goal of this book.

As we go from day to day coping with the ordinary problems of family life, we often seek help from various sources. Some of us turn regularly to authorities on child rearing. With each new book we take from the shelf, we feel a fresh hope that perhaps this one will give us the answers we've been seeking. Often, though, we find that the answers given just don't fit the questions. Have you ever wondered whether it's really some superintelligent baby that's been writing all those child-care books?

Unfortunately, the rules of child rearing frequently lead us only to increased insecurity. Wanting to do a good job, parents try to absorb all the psychology they can. Gradually, they go from ignorance to the happy confidence that comes from knowing the right thing to do in most situations. Then the little tyke breaks a prized possession, and the parent smacks his rear end.

Enter guilt!

What could be more devastating than the haunting awareness that one should have known better? Oh, to be able to wipe away the heinous deed, to reach out and pull back the hand before it strikes! Who knows what psychological damage that blast on the backside might have caused? And even though we reason our way out by telling ourselves that one wallop doesn't make a trauma, we can't quite escape the feeling that we have failed as parents.

This guilt, I am convinced, is one of the major shackles that keeps us from becoming the kind of parents we would like to be. Many of us are haunted by guilt feelings without being aware of their cause. Our enduring self-blame is like a smoldering fire, ever ready to be fanned into a consuming flame by some small mistake. We soon reach the point of being reluctant to try anything new, lest we again slip into incriminating error.

All human beings are subject to making mistakes every

day of our lives. We frequently judge poorly and make unfortunate decisions concerning our children. We are often impatient with them or punish them too severely. Yes, these are mistakes; but they can still have good results.

Making mistakes is, in fact, a part of the learning experience that parents provide for their children. By being able to recognize—and being willing to admit—these mistakes, parents enable their children to see alternative courses of action that may save them many painful moments later in life.

This is not to say that the job most of us do as parents is so good that it can't be improved. Some of the mistakes we make could be avoided if we tried a little harder to be the kind of parents we want to be. It's easy for us to contend that we are, in fact, trying. We invent alibis for our own unfortunate choices, and point to isolated incidents as if they were typical of our constant efforts.

It is here, then, that we as parents find reason to strike our breasts and develop new resolutions. As part of our weak human nature, we have a strong tendency to evil that constantly pulls against the desire to do good. All too often we give in to evil inclinations, or take the easy way out and then rationalize our behavior.

"I've had a very bad day at the office. I'll take Jerry to the movie tomorrow." But tomorrow never comes.

By no means, then, do I intend to suggest that a sense of guilt is always damaging. For our deliberate choices that are contrary to what we know is best, we *should* feel some guilt. But this is a very different matter from the vague self-blame that haunts many of us, usually as a result of repressed experiences of our own childhood. We need to rid ourselves of these continuous guilty feelings, and to accept our parenthood as it has come to be.

CONQUERING INSECURITY

Our children, too, will make mistakes. To try to protect them from these mistakes is to hamper their normal development. God has given them the same freedom we have. Even when they know the right course of action, they have the power to turn away and choose evil. We must not, therefore, hold ourselves accountable for these wrong choices.

Strangely, some parents resist the idea of not being totally responsible for the personality and character development of their children. You'd think we'd appreciate relief from our guilt. But some of us don't want to be relieved if the price we'd have to pay would be a loss of our sense of complete power and control over our children. If something goes wrong in our kids' lives, we had rather it be totally our fault than the effect of forces outside ourselves. If the cause is beyond us, we feel weak and helpless.

For others of us, it's frightening to realize the awesome power we have in our relatively untrained hands. We realize that our influence over our children is lifelong in its impact. We have read about parents' responsibility for developing desirable personality characteristics and the danger of inflicting complexes, hostilities, guilt, inhibitions, and fears on our children.

Understandably, then, we have a natural insecurity that begins almost at the conception of our first child. As we hold the gurgling infants we have procreated, our hands and hearts are often unsteady. And as our growing children encounter the normal problems of life, we grow more painfully aware of our ineptitude. A psychiatrist once asked a patient, "Did it come on rather suddenly, this feeling of being an insignificant pip-squeak? Or did it develop normally with marriage and parenthood?"

We need appreciation—of ourselves and our children—to

help us live with this insecurity. Difficult though it is, we must try to cultivate gratitude for the opportunity to reexperience the maturing process with each of our children. We need to accept the fact that each child is an independent being and that there are many kinds of good and right, not just the kind that our training inclines us to impose on our maturing offspring.

Too often we emphasize what our children should and should not do. We tend to place too much emphasis on caution and not enough on wholehearted living. We tend to think that we are good only if we are miserable, fearful, and negative. It's important, I think, that we clear out of our consciousness the myopic view of morality that is concerned only with the don'ts of life.

Let's take the emphasis off rules, then, and put it on positive appreciation and generous giving. Give yourself the freedom to enjoy a proud parenthood and help your offspring free themselves for full enjoyment of childhood.

AS YOU ARE NOW

Try to appreciate yourself as you are now, and resolve to move ahead to the quality of life you choose. Successful parenting requires no unusual talents or sophisticated training. You have what it takes.

You have what it takes to deal with most of the everyday problems. One mother wrote to the pediatrician: "We're having difficulty with our daughter in a few small areas—sleeping, eating, toilet training, and behavior. Otherwise, everything's fine."

You have what it takes to live most of your days without panic. A Wisconsin newspaper carried this ad: "Frantic mother wants time-consuming items with lots of nuts and bolts for small boy to destroy. Or, will trade small boy."

In the chapters ahead I'll talk about some of the problems

confronting nearly every parent. My main concern is to help you to see these everyday difficulties in proper perspective and to use them as stepping-stones to freedom. Success as a parent is "in the cards" for you; don't let it get lost in the shuffle.

Like every other parent that ever lived, you'll have good days and you'll have bad. You'll have days when your heart aches with compassion and days when it pounds with angry frustration. You'll have days when the thoughtless back talk or the forgotten birthday brings the almost intolerable pain of not being appreciated.

But nursing those wounds will have to wait. You've got to hurry along now to show your child the rainbow.

CHAPTER 3

A SHORT INVENTORY

KNOWING AND FEELING

Trouble is, when we say that parents and kids are good for each other, it brings back memories of what Mom used to tell us about spinach—or the way she used to pretend to sip that nauseating medicine and then lick her lips to convince us that it tasted like ice cream.

If you're experiencing a castor-oil parenthood, you're not really ready to believe anybody who tries to tell you how delightful raising kids can be. And the "kids are good for you" theme probably sounds like an alley cat's aria.

For some of us it's easy to understand that parenthood is a wonderful gift from God, something we should be proud of in a strongly positive, constructive way. But *knowing* that this is so doesn't do much to help us *feel* proud or richly blessed. Instead, we are weighted down by responsibility, worry, and frustration.

Being proud of our parenthood entails being proud of the people involved in it. This means we have to take pride in our children, even with all their human frailties (OK, call them stupid mistakes if you must). It also means taking pride in ourselves—for what God has made us—and this is often the most difficult challenge of all.

Show-and-tell time, the most joked about period in school life, is a time for kids to present things they're proud of. We need a moderate amount of show-and-tell time for our parenthood, to let us talk about the events of family life that we take pride in.

To clarify why we don't allow ourselves this, let me add to the storehouse of show-and-tell humor. One day when Wendy was going through some junk in the basement, she found her father's dog tags, the metal identification that had hung from a chain around his neck throughout his army days. After some coquettish persuasion, Dad let her take them to kindergarten for show and tell. "These," she boasted, "were my daddy's tags. He used to have to keep them on all the time when he was a dog."

Well, fellow ex-canines, our dog days are over (no offense to national defense). It's time to give up our tail-between-the-legs behavior and start feeling good about what we have and what we are. Let's take a good, honest look at ourselves. Let's get to know ourselves better. The depth of our self-knowledge determines how we handle different situations, how we react to others, and how we want to be treated.

In striving for more complete self-knowledge, we will also uncover many personal strengths. We all have them. It's important that we gain an awareness of our strong qualities in order to move forward toward our goals. The relationship of seeing our strengths to taking pride in our parenthood is obvious; but we should also be aware that we need to know our strengths in order to build on them.

A STARTING POINT

In the chapters ahead, I want to help you discover some of your strengths. One of the most astounding surprises of self-discovery is that our strongest qualities are so much like our least desirable traits. There is no human characteristic that does not include some potential for good. Often, we can convert what seems like a weakness to a point of particular strength.

Difficult as self-knowledge is, we all have some. Living constantly with ourselves, we cannot help but discover a great deal of what we are. Even our most effective forms of self-deception do not shield us completely from coming to know ourselves.

Typically, it's not through introspection or self-inquiry that we find out about ourselves. Rather, as we meet and interact with others and disclose parts of ourselves to them, we grow in our self-knowledge. Still, from time to time it's good for us to pause and take inventory of the kind of people we really are. As we hold a mirror up to our inner selves and take stock of our dominant characteristics, we often become more able to move forward to becoming what we want to be.

To give you an opportunity for a quick self-inventory, the next page presents a list of twenty-five characteristics that have something to do with the content of the rest of the book. Before you read on, you might want to select from this list the five words that you think best describe you. Opposite each word is a letter that corresponds to a certain numbered score. Give yourself five points for each *a* word, four for each *b*, three for each *c*, two for each *d*, and one for each *e*. Then find your place on the scale following the list.

Be as honest as you can in choosing your answers. An opportunity for a more thorough self-inventory is offered in the Appendix.

___ Angry - b   ___ Negligent - e
___ Argumentative - c   ___ Passive - e
___ Bad-Tempered - b   ___ Punitive - a
___ Defensive - c   ___ Rigid - a
___ Excitable - b   ___ Soft-Touch - d
___ Fainthearted - e   ___ Stern - a
___ Fickle - d   ___ Strict - a
___ Harsh - a   ___ Submissive - d
___ Impatient - b   ___ Unconcerned - e
___ Inadequate - c   ___ Uneasy - c
___ Indifferent - e   ___ Yielding - d
___ Insecure - c   ___ Wishy-Washy - d
___ Irritable - b

	Passive	Submissive	Neutral (Possibly Defensive)	Angry	Punitive
	5	10	15	20	25
KEY:	⌊_____	_____	_____	_____	_____⌋

CHAPTER 4

QUICK TO PUNISH?
BREAK YOUR OWN CHAINS

PUNITIVE PARENTS

Many parents beat up their kids. You've probably read about "the battered child." Every year fifty thousand or so American parents are apprehended for child abuse. It isn't likely that you've been one of them—but how close have you come?

Why are we so quick to punish our children when they disobey us or otherwise go against our will? Why aren't we more patient? Sometimes it's almost as if we have no control over our impulses. We seem to be enslaved by our emotional reactions and by deeply rooted, habitual response patterns.

Just for a moment, though, try to remember some instance when you succeeded in responding more helpfully to your child. If you had to struggle to restrain yourself, you almost certainly felt some initial frustration. But then, as the anger melted, you probably experienced some pleasure in knowing that you had scored a victory. You were proud of your success.

This victorious feeling can be yours more often. In time it can become the rule rather than the exception. Take advantage of today's opportunity to break out of the chains that enslave you. Start by looking honestly at your reactions and sincerely trying to understand them.

I remember an educational toy of a few years ago that consisted of five steel balls suspended by string. When one or more of these balls were drawn back and released, they would swing into the others and force off an equal number of balls on the opposite end.

Although this toy was designed to illustrate a principle of physics, it also has a meaning for us. There's a parallel psychological phenomenon that explains why we often act more punitively toward our children than the importance of the situation warrants. Frustration or misfortune affects us as a kind of punishment, and we respond in like fashion toward our kids.

Most punitive parents had punitive parents; and their children, when grown, are also likely to overpunish their children. An so it goes from generation to generation, just as if a long series of those same toys were placed side by side.

BREAKING THE CHAIN

How do we break this chain? How do we halt the transmittal of punitive attitudes and habits from generation to generation? Let yourself be honest and vulnerable.

First, we need to be honest. Bringing our attitudes out into the open is important.

It's usually difficult for us to recognize our punitive attitudes toward ourselves. Without being aware of it, we go on inflicting on ourselves the scolding and deprivation we have been used to. We fail to see this self-punishment eroding our ability to enjoy life. Least of all do we connect our treatment of our kids with how we were treated as children.

We need to be able to look beyond the incident of the moment that brings us to the point of inflicting punishment, and to see the cumulation of events in our past life that have conditioned us to react as we do. Inevitably, we see our offspring as reflections or extensions of ourselves. For most of us, the child offers a hope of self-realization. Kept within bounds, this hope can be a strongly positive influence in cementing the relationship of parent to child.

Too often, though, the parent wants the child to have all the good qualities he sees in himself, plus many personal strengths that have remained beyond the parent's reach. One struggling student remarked, "My dad wants me to have all the things he didn't have as a child—like all A's on my report card."

Typically, instead of the image of perfection we look for in our children, we see a reflection of some of our most troubling weaknesses. Because we have not been able to accept these characteristics in ourselves, their reflection interferes with full acceptance of our children.

Things our children do frequently recall past feelings and conflicts in us. We remember events of our childhood, and we tend to react as our parents did toward us.

Evangelist Grady Wilson was asked whether his mother ever spanked him. He responded, "Did she ever spank me! She had a strap in the kitchen hanging under the motto, 'I need thee every hour!'"

Punishment, of course, is not necessarily physical. The term includes corporal punishment, but it also extends to other forms of "corrective" action such as disapproval, blame, and censure. Words, and even silence, can be just as punitive as the most severe whipping.

Punishment generally carries with it the idea of penalty,

pain, or loss. It may take an active form, like spanking, scolding, or sending to bed. It may be deprivation of some privilege or pleasure, like toys, candy, or recreation. Or it may consist of repeated, strict moralizing, creating feelings of guilt and worthlessness in the child. Each kind of punishment brings its own kind of hurt.

It isn't necessary, or generally helpful, to review the horrid details of each specific past incident. What is important is the simple realization that our feelings are linked to the past. Then, even though we didn't invite them into our present lives, we can accept them as legitimate. I'll have more to say in the next two chapters about the importance of this acceptance.

LIMITING PRESENT IMPACT

Most important of all, recognizing that these feelings belong to the past prepares us to limit their impact on present actions. We might resist the urge to hit a child and instead look for a more constructive form of discipline. We might admit that a punishment already prescribed is too severe and then modify it to suit the child's need rather than our own. Or we might simply have greater confidence as we renew our resolution to be more rational.

Enabling us to limit the effects of feelings from the past is perhaps the chief contribution of transactional analysis. This popular psychological approach distinguishes responses that come from our three "selves": child, parent, adult. As we strive to replace spontaneous child and parent reactions with those that come from the adult in us, we come ever closer to keeping the past in its proper place.

When you deliberately set out to prevent past feelings from interfering with present happiness, you can expect some difficulty. The task requires patience and hard work. It would be much easier to coast along in the same familiar patterns. As you make changes in your customary behavior, you'll often feel a strong pull toward your old attitudes.

In fact, the new forms of response are likely to seem somewhat unnatural to you. You may feel like saying, "I just can't do that," or "I'm not that kind of person." You're right, of course. And the choice will always be yours—to remain the kind of person you are or to move toward what you want to be.

The anxiety that sometimes comes with attempts to change is a sign of progress. If you feel consistently at home with yourself, you can be rather sure that your behavior is not changing significantly. But if you experience feelings of inner strangeness, you are probably making considerable gains in changing the pattern of your responses.

The feelings of strangeness will fade in time. You'll recognize and appreciate the benefits you're deriving from your new behavior. You'll become more accustomed to your changing attitudes. And you'll be much happier with yourself as you strip away the constant inclination to punish your child.

ARE YOU OVERDOING IT?

OK, so you don't beat your child every day. You may still wonder whether you inflict punishment more often than you should. Perhaps reading the last chapter has led you to think you do. But it's hard to tell. Even if you could sit down with a psychologist and discuss the matter, it would be difficult to judge the appropriateness of your disciplinary techniques. The truth is that no one else knows your son or daughter as well as you do. No one else experiences the day-to-day situation in your home. And no one else can really say what kind of action is called for by the things that happen where you live.

You can compare notes, though. You can talk to friends

and neighbors about their children's behavior (but don't expect them to be always honest). You can discuss the kinds of discipline parents apply (keeping in mind they won't tell you about all the things they do when they lose control). If you haven't been engaging in occasional discussion about such matters, look for an opportunity to start.

I do want to tell you what I know about the usual effects of punishment. What I want you to remember about this information, though, is that it might not fit your situation perfectly. You have to try it on for size. And deciding whether it fits may bring more than a little discomfort (never did get into those smaller-sized shoes, did you?).

Mostly I want you to be free to choose the disciplinary approach that's most appropriate for you and your children. If you use punishment because you sincerely believe it's the best tactic for your situation, it might work very well. By being honest with yourself, you can move toward a more joyful parenthood.

REVIEW YOUR RULES

A starting point in evaluating your disciplinary strategies is reviewing what you expect of your child. What are the rules you expect him to follow?

Let's define a rule as any statement intended to guide conduct on more than one specific occasion. In their ideal form, rules represent the application of tested values the family subscribes to. We'll say more about values later. In general, though, the wise parent keeps the number of rules he sets to a minimum. He avoids the clutter that results from trying to prescribe correct conduct for a wide variety of specific instances.

A rule may be necessary, for instance, to insure that children who take music lessons also take the trouble to practice—if that's really important. But first ask *why* the children should practice. Our daughter had been taking piano lessons only a short while when she first played Beethoven. Beethoven lost. Still, we knew she had talent, and using that talent well seemed important. On this basis we established a rule to insure daily practice. Today she plays very proficiently, practicing almost every chance she gets.

For a son with less natural inclination, our value focus has been on the use of financial resources. Our rule is that he pays for his own lesson with paper route money if he chooses not to practice. He enjoys taking lessons and playing in the band. And the teacher feels his progress is satisfactory even if he doesn't always practice.

No better guidance could be offered parents in setting family rules than this quotation from the Torah: "Don't make a fence that is more important [expensive] than what is fenced in" (Midr. Gen. Rab. 19:3). Rules are important to the child, but they should never be made or enforced for their own sakes.

INSURING UNDERSTANDING

Secondly, be sure to communicate your rules clearly. If a rule is worth making, it needs to be clearly understood. Children need to be informed of rules in a way that will not be taken as criticism. Imagine a set of game rules that begins, "What's the matter with you, you dummy? Don't you know how to play this game?" It's a good idea to accompany every interpretation of a rule with some sign of affection.

Communication of rules is not, of course, a one-time effort. We must all discover the rules of family and social living gradually. Referee Tom Thorpe once put a football player out of the game for using foul language. He had given the angered gridder repeated warnings but to no avail. Finally he ejected him.

"What rule did I violate?" the player asked heatedly.

"What rule did he violate?" echoed his coach and teammates.

Thorpe stared at them for a moment and then answered calmly, "The Golden Rule."

The parent's role in communicating rules resembles that of the experienced teacher who does more guiding of individual discovery than lecturing. Maybe you can recall the confused feeling of childhood that came with being scolded when you had no sense of having done wrong. To some extent this is an inevitable part of developing a conscience. As the child grows, however, he becomes more able to understand the rules of the game—and more entitled to know them.

Have you ever been in a deuces-wild poker game that you thought was straight? Or, did you ever play Monopoly not knowing that house rules said you had to *ask for* your $200 for passing Go? (Has it really gone up to $400?) Before you finish your move, the next player grabs the dice, rolls, and laughs, "You didn't call it!"

It's easy to err in assuming that children understand rules. My son wanted a set of barbells. After much persuasion I bought them for him. Now he develops his muscles lifting weights while his mother strains her back carrying out the garbage cans. When I'm available to relieve my wife of this burden, I'm vividly aware that this should be my sons' responsibility. As I review the situation, though, I'm not at all sure that I've ever defined this responsibility clearly for them. I think we often make this mistake— assuming that we have clearly communicated our wishes when the message has really never been sent. Or perhaps we've sent it at a time when reception lines were not open.

As with every other aspect of parenthood, you have to have faith in your ability to use common sense. The two-year-old who happily announces that he's helped you by peeling all the bananas for next week's lunches is the victim of insufficient information. But when the kindergarten child protests, "You didn't say I wasn't allowed to iron marshmallows," credibility wanes.

WHAT PUNISHMENT DOES

After rules are made and communicated, there comes the need for enforcement. Ever since human beings began to live in communities, they have recognized this need. But somewhere along the line the emphasis changed. Laws and rules came to be made and enforced so as to keep the ruler in power rather than to protect man from man. The ruler made the law. Therefore, the law was good, and anyone who broke the law was to be punished. The motive changed from protective to punitive.

Tragically, this seems to describe the outlook of many parents. We claim to seek the good of the child, to be interested in teaching him respect and discipline. In reality, we are driven by a subconscious desire to reinforce our feelings of power.

This is punishment's greatest success. If we start early enough, even the skimpiest parent can prove that he or she has more physical strength than the child. And to some of us, that's important.

There are also some secondary benefits to the punisher. Tension may be relieved, for example. Or we might stop some behavior of the child that has been making our life miserable.

But only temporarily. Punishment has almost no long-term effect on behavior. If it were effective, our society would long since have been rid of criminals, juvenile delinquents, and bratty kids. On the contrary, the undesirable behavior nearly always resurfaces—with greater vigor and determination than ever.

There are occasional exceptions, however. Once in a while we find that a few consistent applications of mild punishment do result in a fairly permanent inhibition of an undesirable behavior. A child who has been slapped a few times for stepping off the curb may begin to stay on the sidewalk. This punishment has served merely to inform the child that the behavior is unacceptable. It's the desire to please the parent and the parent's approval of not stepping off the curb that maintain the inhibition, not the fear of punishment.

OTHER EFFECTS

Punishment also has the disadvantage of causing the punished person to resent and dislike the one who punishes. The punisher thus becomes less effective in future discipline. He becomes a figure the child wishes to defy or avoid rather than obey.

"You'll be sorry," one lad said to his mother when she sent him to his room. "People will ask me, 'How's your mother?' and I'll say, 'Mean!'" And to his father he said: "Don't ever call me Pal again. People don't make their pals sit in a lousy corner."

Punishment also makes it more difficult for the child to love himself. Being punished tends to create a negative self-image, a failure identity. No child is encouraged to see value in himself and to do better when we beat him over the head with his mistakes and failures. He merely becomes more discouraged. He wouldn't misbehave in the first place if (through positive and useful behavior) he felt he could have a sense of worthwhileness and be seen as a valuable person.

Punishment can also foster pretense. Unfortunately,

most of us parents are upset when a child openly admits bad intentions. Therefore, the child learns to make good excuses. If he drops a vase, Mother accepts the apology, "Sorry, it slipped out of my hand." Often a truer explanation would be that the child was angry and resentful. But his fear of being punished leads the child to seek excuses rather than express his real feelings and intentions. Then there is created an inner conflict, and his intentions and sense of guilt become intolerable.

This self-defeating pattern robs the child of the freedom to grow and of the strength and encouragement he needs to assume responsibility for his own behavior.

Self-excuse and dodging of responsibility are not what we want to cultivate in our children. We want our children to be able to face reality and accept themselves for what they are. We want the kind of sincerity shown by the seven-year-old who prayed, "Dear God, I'm a pretty good Christian, but I'm a better shortstop."

The strict, harshly punitive environment of many homes cultivates both self-hatred and a desire for revenge in children. Continuously put down, the child quickly loses self-respect, without being aware of why he dislikes himself. On the conscious level, he is more likely to respond revengefully. "Go ahead, keep putting me down now. Treat me like a worthless animal. But just wait till I get bigger and stronger."

Such a reaction almost inevitably makes the child feel more guilty. As a result, he hates himself even more. No wonder the effects of excessive punishment survive to be passed on to our children's children!

WHY CHILDREN SEEK PUNISHMENT
Children often appear to be deliberately seeking punishment. Why is this?

One of the most common reasons is the child's own sense of guilt. Punishment relieves the guilt, and this is less painful to the child than his own self-torture. It is common for children to have a "bookkeeping" sense of justice, which requires that every misdeed incurs a retaliation. Parents often foster this attitude through punishment.

Or the child may be seeking punishment for a lesser crime, hoping to ease his guilt for what he considers a more serious offense. Perhaps Raymond feels intense hatred toward his little brother. Because he considers this feeling evil, however, he pushes it out of his conscious awareness. His guilt feelings are only vaguely defined, and yet he has need of relief. Under the pressure of this need he misbehaves and earns punishment from his parents. At least for the moment, then, he relieves his sense of guilt over the repressed, more serious misbehavior.

At times, punishment can be a pleasurable experience for the child. Fear of punishment creates tension; this tension is relieved when the punishment is inflicted. And there is pleasure in the relief.

But perhaps the most common reason why children seek punishment is simply a need for attention. All of us need the assurance that comes from having others pay attention to us. Some children are so starved for attention that even the pain of severe punishment is an oasis compared to the barrenness of being ignored. They come to the conclusion that if they can't get affection or approval, they'll settle for what's available. If they aren't successful in gaining favorable attention, they'll settle for punishment.

I hope these few facts help you understand a little better why your children sometimes behave as they do. I hope, too, that you'll take an honest look at your own feelings and at the events from your past that impel you to react in certain ways toward your children. By evaluating your disciplinary techniques, making sure that your rules are clearly defined and understood, you may find it possible to gain obedience and cooperation without constantly relying on punishment.

In every parent's life, though, there comes the coolly calculated plan that goes awry. One mother, tired of the constant disorder in her sons' room, got the boys to agree that they would pay her a penny for every item she had to pick up in their room. At the end of the week, they owed her twenty-seven cents. She received the twenty-seven cents, plus a dime tip, with a note saying: "Thanks, Mom. Keep up the good work!"

CHAPTER 5

OFTEN ANGRY? EXPLODE WITH LOVE

THE PROBLEM OF ANGER

Some of us have short fuses. Despite repeated resolutions to the contrary, we find ourselves getting angry at just about everything. When things don't go right in our lives, our frustration level is much higher than we would like it to be.

What an opportunity to bring pride to your parenthood!

These same strong feelings that push at our insides to be released when things go wrong can be a strong positive force. The world's most volatile people also have the most energy to invest in the service of love. It's a simple conversion, and you can start it right now.

If you find yourself getting angry often, the first step is to try to understand your anger. Then you can move on to increasing your power over your feelings. This will put you in a position to decide when and how to expend this precious energy. Rather than squandering it and doing things you'll regret later, you will be able to use your anger for good purposes.

First, tackle understanding. Learning more about the causes and nature of anger will remove some of the mystery. Soon you'll no longer have to say, "I don't know why I get so worked up. I wish I could control myself a little more."

Let's start by discussing things that make us angry. Many different kinds of situations can arouse angry feelings—often without our being aware of what's happening. For instance, we sometimes get angry at the things we depend on to do our work or to have fun (they just don't make 'em like they used to!).

I know it's ridiculous to holler at my bowling ball for not going where I try to send it. Really, that stupid ball has no control over its trajectory. It can't do anything about the poorly kept alleys that keep it from breaking into the pocket. Of course, once in a while (maybe eight or nine frames a game), I just might not throw the ball exactly right.

Besides getting angry at things, we often get angry at people, too. Sometimes these are the people who are nearest and dearest. Did you ever spend four weeks in a station wagon with those you thought you loved best? At times, the situations we get ourselves into tax our human control system to the point of tyranny.

Every child, of course, does many things that stir up anger in parents. Let's face it. It *is* difficult for a mother to be calmly acceptant when the first-grader rouses her from sleep just after midnight with: "Mom, I forgot to tell you. You have to make me a soldier's costume for the school play tomorrow."

PERSONAL THREATS

Sometimes the causes of anger are obvious. A child may seem determined to arouse our wrath. He begins by banging two pans together and goes as far as necessary to get a reaction, even if it means letting the bathtub run over. Just as often, though, it's a rather subtle matter that stirs us to anger—perhaps some minor personal threat. Imagine, for example, this conversation:

"Dad, help me with my homework."

"Sure. I guess a guy who's a PTA officer should be able to put the newspaper aside long enough to give his daughter a helping hand."

"That's great, Dad."

"Oh, you're doing math, huh? Yeah, this new math is kind of tricky. Well, let's see . . . You know, we were discussing this homework thing at the PTA meeting last week. You kids have to learn to stand on your own two feet. I can't always be helping you out of jams. If you'd pay attention in class, you'd understand this stuff. Work it out for yourself!"

In-verse Opportunity

My father's a peace-loving creature
Who shows no impatience or wrath.
He's a kindly, benevolent teacher—
Till I ask him for help with my math.

Our own sense of inadequacy is often the source of our strongest anger. We all need to feel able to handle the events that arise in our lives. This is why emotional outbursts often cause more problems than they solve. We end up being very angry with ourselves for not having better control.

Common to nearly all situations that arouse us to anger is the single element of threat to one's ego. This threat may take the form of feelings that we have been injured, criticized unjustly, humiliated, or rejected. Intensity may range from mild annoyance to uncontrollable fury. But the closer the threat comes to the center of our ego, the more intense the feeling will be. Among the most threatening, most anger-provoking experiences for a parent, for example, is failure to correct a flaw in a child's behavior that mirrors a weakness of the parent himself.

Very often, the person or thing we take our anger out on is not the same as what provokes us. We tend to find safe outlets. My bowling ball can't feel inadequate and hate itself as I can. Our children can't get back at us as readily as our spouses or business associates can—usually.

But there's still a haunting awareness that we have lost control, acted foolishly, and perhaps hurt someone we love. This knowledge is likely to motivate us to remedy the problem. Once we see the causes of our anger more clearly, we can begin to move in that direction. We have an opportunity to begin counteracting the anger with positive thoughts about whatever it is that provokes us.

WHAT HAPPENS

A second kind of understanding that helps us gain control is knowing what happens when we're angry. For the clearest realization of this, you might want to hold your breath while you read this section. That's it—take a deep breath and hold it.

Once angry feelings occur, they seem to be self-nurturing. Your favorite problem child does something wrong. You correct him, perhaps a little more sharply than you should. The child comes back at you in the same tone. You do him one better.

As the angry feelings swell within you, physical changes take place. Your rate of metabolism changes. Noradrenalin is released into your bloodstream, and your senses are alerted and finely tuned. Your blood vessels expand, and your breathing and heart rate quicken. There is an increase in blood sugar concentration, resulting in a spurt of energy. Your body feels that it must do *something,* regardless of what the circumstances might be.

It goes pretty much the same with everybody. Something happens that sets off an emotional reaction. A son or daughter defies you; your spouse criticizes a point of particular sensitivity; a friend stubbornly disagrees with you on some important issue. You feel an urge to lash out. If the urge is beyond your control, you slap or shake the child, you thrust the blade of your most cutting insult into your spouse or friend. You pound the table. You slam a door. You hurl a book on the floor.

That's anger. By now, though, you've probably given up holding your breath. Or, if you're a speed reader or controlled breather, you're probably wondering how much longer you should hold. In any case, you'll eventually *have* to let go. Sooner or later you must yield to the need to breathe.

So go ahead. Take a breath—and gain an insight. The need to express the feelings that are aroused by ego-threat is as inescapable as the need to breathe. Just as the speed reader could absorb more material before breathing, so also the person with a strong ego could tolerate more threat. Just as the controlled breather could wait longer before breathing, so also one who has developed temper control could restrain himself for a longer period. But everyone has to breathe to survive physically, and everyone has to express angry feelings to survive emotionally.

Accept your anger, then, as a natural human emotion. Rid yourself of the idea that anger is immoral. As a child you may have been made to feel guilty for hostile feelings. You may have been led to believe that feeling angry meant not having self-control.

Now you find yourself often trying too hard to be patient. You keep feelings pent up inside yourself so long that sooner or later you explode. Or, you might sometimes even deny your anger, saying things like, "I'm not mad" or "I'm not going to get emotional about this," while the anger swells inside you.

SUPPRESS OR EXPRESS?

Suppressing anger can be hazardous to your health. The physical changes that occur when you're angry are so rapid and numerous that your health is jeopardized when the tension is not released. If suppressing anger is part of one's life-style, it can lead to chronic hypertension. Asthma attacks, migraine headaches, and allergies have been traced to such causes. Doctors also believe that suppressed anger can increase susceptibility to colds and cause chronic back and neck pains.

These unreleased feelings sometimes keep us awake at night. They can lead us gradually to a sense of hopelessness. And they can dull us to the point where we cannot fully experience more pleasant, sustaining emotions.

Anger that is submerged becomes harder to express appropriately. Its sources are increasingly harder to recognize. We need to find ways to express these feelings at the time they originally occur.

NEED FOR CONTROL

But you can't go on continually raising the roof. People will begin to think there's something wrong in your attic. Try raising just your eyebrows for a change.

You need to steer your life away from physical violence, verbal attacks, and psychological abuse. Name-calling, destructive criticism, sarcasm, harsh accusations—these expressions of angry feelings you'd be better off without.

You'd be happier, too, if you never kicked or threw another object or slammed another door. So would the people around you.

Let's not kid ourselves. Some of the means we use to vent our anger are not nearly as automatic or spontaneous as we'd like to believe. Slamming doors—or even people—can be a very deliberate action. The same is true of throwing things. After all, the object we throw doesn't just jump into our hand.

Anger can also be merely a manipulative counterfeit. This is a fancy way of saying that we sometimes get mad at our kids just to scare them, to get them to do what we want. By shouting or screaming, we create fear that causes them to do our will—and to turn a little farther away from us.

However deliberate our angry actions might be, restraint is often necessary. We have an obligation to protect others from our anger. This is particularly important at peak moments of rage. Although some psychologists maintain that it is sometimes good to give full expression to our anger, I believe it is better to maintain control than to risk injuring those around us. The consequences of giving in to anger include so much potential for hurt and insult that it can hardly be worth the danger involved.

Further, if we frequently indulge our anger, it tends to get worse instead of better. With increasing frequency, it seeks new and sharper ways of inflicting personal injury. There is a lessening of respect and a tendency toward dislike or hatred.

Most often when we have succeeded in controlling our emotions, we experience a gain in self-respect. We come away pleased that we have maintained self-control. By contrast, our uncontrolled explosions tend to leave us with feelings of regret as well as damaged interpersonal relationships.

In general, then, family members might best seek to follow a rule that says: "Don't give way to anger at one another. Learn to control the actions that result from angry feelings. Avoid inflicting insult and injury on children, spouse, parents."

It may be helpful to recognize some of the situations that tend to produce the strongest feelings of anger. If these situations cannot be avoided, we can at least prepare ourselves to maintain adequate control.

If you feel yourself starting to boil every time you pass your son's incredibly cluttered room, it might help to keep the door shut. Or you might simply resolve again to be calm as you hand him the rake and tell him to get busy cleaning it up.

Hopeless disorder seems to be a universal characteristic of boys' rooms:

"Mom, my right shoe is lost."

"That's ridiculous. How could it be lost. Just stop and think; where did you take it off last night?"

"In my room."

"It's lost."

THE LIMITS OF RESTRAINT

Understanding your anger can help you deal with it; so can a resolution to control it. But these remedies reach only so far, especially on those bad days when everything goes awry. Expressing anger *is* essential.

But expressing doesn't have to mean exploding—at least not in the face of those we love. We need to find constructive outlets for our feelings. We need to seek the best ways of using our emotions. We need to express our emotions without shaming our children, embarrassing, frightening, or exploiting them.

If properly directed, anger can be a valuable means of bringing people together. Perls has said that anger is a sympathetic feeling. Especially when this emotion includes genuine concern for another, anger can be used to break down the barriers that block communication.

RECOGNIZING FEELINGS

An essential first step is recognizing our own true feelings. This can be hard. Even when we resolve to be honest with ourselves, we often have to struggle to see our feelings objectively. We find it difficult to accept certain feelings in ourselves and tend to try convincing ourselves that they do not exist.

Most of us grow to adulthood having some tendency toward perfectionism. Even though we may be able to admit some of our shortcomings, we cannot rid ourselves of the feeling that we must do everything perfectly. Instead of using this drive as a means of motivation toward self-improvement, we let it push us toward discouragement and denial of some of our less admirable feelings.

What father, for example, could be honest about his feelings when his son bounces on his stomach and then suggests, "Maybe you should go on a diet, Dad; your stomach's starting to feel squooshy!"

It is also possible to acknowledge feelings of anger but suppress any awareness of who aroused them or why. We may believe that the source of our feelings is something quite different from the real origin. The longer we keep our emotions and their causes under wraps, the more difficult it becomes to see them accurately.

It takes a great deal of courage and persistence, then, to let our fugitive selves emerge. It takes a lot of testing and dipping our toes into the water to attain any reasonable degree of self-knowledge. It is worth the effort, though, because this is the only real way we can know who we are and communicate this to the outside world. It's worth the struggle to ward off the consistent tendency to self-deception. It's worth the resolution again and again to be completely honest with ourselves.

The effort must be deliberate. You may have to call a quiet time-out just to get in touch with your real emotions. It's sometimes helpful to write down the adjectives that best describe the way you feel. Then, try to group them under some one general mood. The mood might be anger, but it could just as easily be melancholy or anxiety.

What are some of the most common feelings your children stir up in you? Discomfort? Displeasure? Annoyance? Irritation? Frustration? Exasperation? Indignation? Dismay? Fury? You are entitled to these feelings without shame or guilt.

Holding ourselves morally responsible for our feelings is a serious mistake. Feelings, by their nature, are unbidden and somewhat unpredictable. The word "should" has nothing to do with feelings. "Should" speaks only to the will.

ADMITTING ANGER

Once we realize fully that we are not responsible for our feelings, we find it easier to admit it when anger comes on. Then we are likely to be more successful in fulfilling our moral responsibility for what we *do* about these feelings. In most situations the ideal is to express our feelings when they first occur and in the direction of the person who caused them. To be able to say, "I just won't stand for that!" and follow through on that expression of feeling gives one the realization that it is possible to get angry effectively. If we let the person who makes us angry know our feelings right away, this person will usually be apologetic and want to remain our friend.

A parent, then, should not hesitate to admit, "Your refusal to do as you're told makes me angry." Then, under the force of the same emotion, he or she can look toward better understanding: "Help me understand why you don't want to obey."

Our expressions of anger must be factual and straightforward. As objectively as possible, we try to translate our feelings into words without moralizing or philosophizing. There should be no verbal additions to the simplest words that can reflect how we feel. "I'm furious" does the job very well, and all that remains is to make sure the child understands what it is that stirred up this emotion.

The social situation in which we find ourselves has a strong influence on how well we recognize our feelings and how freely we express them. Sometimes people we are with or the conditions under which an event occurs make it difficult for us to know how to feel. Even when we are clear about our own emotions, it isn't always best to express them openly. A person who is likely to lose his job if his boss discovers his true feelings is better off finding some other way to "get it out of his system."

With our children, though, obstacles should be fewer. If we make a reasonable effort to keep a degree of openness in our relationship, we should be able to let our children know how we feel without taking serious risk.

Unfortunately, many people see little difference between word and action. In their minds, admitting one's anger toward a person is equivalent to attacking that person. It doesn't have to be. If we take care to be as objective as possible in describing our feelings, we can express them without inflicting hurt on those around us.

Under no circumstances does admitting our anger mean we need to take physical action. Only a psychopath has to act on every feeling regardless of consequences. Just letting yourself know your real feelings (no matter how freakish they might seem) is excellent insurance against their taking command of you and causing you to act in a way you'll regret.

CONSTRUCTIVE OUTLETS

When we do find it necessary or expedient to withhold verbal expression of anger, we must discover other kinds of outlets for our feelings. This is a universal need.

There is value in "letting off steam." We can do this by slamming a golf ball, mowing a lawn, singing in the shower, or even painting a picture. Our personal inclinations and the intensity of our feelings will guide us toward more acceptable outlets.

Not all of these indirect means of expressing anger are constructive. Recently I saw a newspaper item about two men who used paintbrushes to express their anger. One, a California man, painted a huge face on the side of his neighbor's house—and had the face sticking its tongue out at the neighbor when he came home from vacation. Much more conservatively, an ecologist expressed his displeasure at the destruction of trees for highway construction by altering a sign to read. "Your Highway Axes at Work."

On the other hand, the "People Are Funny" TV show once featured a man whose job it was to smash defective dishes. While he was being interviewed on stage, he threw plates, cups, and saucers against a cement wall, just as he might do on his job. This man assured the emcee that he had never quarreled with his wife, children, or neighbors because he managed to get rid of his violent feelings before he got home each night.

One constructive technique that can often be employed to get rid of angry feelings is the expression of humor. Some parents find it easy to laugh at their own emotional reactions. A joke or a harmless touch of humor can do much to defuse pent-up anger.

For instance, a mother waiting impatiently for her adolescent son to get ready for church might very well begin to enjoy her own impatience. Someone has said that the person who doubts the principle of perpetual motion has never seen a fifteen-year-old comb his hair. Mom might remember that just a few years ago, she was constantly upset by the fact that her son's hair was never in place.

Using humor to relieve angry feelings does not mean laughing at our children—either at their immaturity or their cuteness. It is far better to make fun of ourselves or of the situation in which we find ourselves.

The refusal of a four-year-old to get ready to go outside can be exasperating. You might recognize your beginning anger and grab the child's coat with the same vigor that you're tempted to grab his throat. Holding up a sleeve you might say, "Let's see now. Your leg must go in here somewhere." There's no guarantee, of course, that such an approach will get the child dressed more quickly. But it will help to minimize your frustration.

Some adults believe that having fun with children is childish. On the contrary, a sense of humor is a distinct mark of maturity. No child is mature enough to laugh at himself habitually. Only adults can see the humor in many of life's difficult situations.

Humor provides a direct means of communicating with children. It promotes mutual respect and understanding. Adults who are able to keep one eye on the humorous elements of their relationships with children will find the bonds growing stronger as adult and child grow together.

SHORT REVIEW

The important thing is to make the means we use to express our anger as constructive as possible. The man who vents his feelings by angrily hammering nails to build a woodshed is better off than the man who uses an ax to demolish one. Even if the woodshed has outlived its usefulness, the man who destroys it will not have the satisfaction of admiring his handiwork when his feelings have been released.

Any expression of feelings, though, is better than holding them in—as long as what we do does not injure another or ourselves. Keeping feelings inside will lead to emotional or physical difficulties. It will also eventually result in an explosive release that is beyond the control of reason.

We need to work at developing patience. This includes reminding ourselves to keep calm and fully enjoying those occasions on which we are successful. We need to anticipate the circumstances that stir up the most anger in us, and either avoid them or make the necessary preparations for handling them.

In spite of our best efforts to develop self-control, all of us occasionally blow up. Perhaps your objective is to go seven complete days without erupting. You sincerely look for constructive ways to express your anger. Then, on the sixth day, you get the "Who are you to tell me what to do?" routine from your know-it-all teen-ager. Things go out of control. My advice at such a time is, "When your brakes fail, try to hit something cheap."

CHAPTER 6

READY TO FIGHT? SHAKE HANDS WITH THE REAL YOU

ON THE DEFENSIVE

Christmas Eve. A time of joyous harmony and family unity, right? Well, not necessarily.

My thoughts go back to a Christmas Eve of several years ago and an incident I would surely have repressed from memory if I hadn't written it down. I guess I knew I'd have to tell the world about it someday.

The whole thing might not have happened if I didn't believe in the importance of family unity. But we have this rule that says that the family goes to church *together*. Now that we have young adults in the family, we exempt them if they prefer to go at a different time. And, of course, we've always made exceptions for a good cause—by *our* criteria.

The cause wasn't good enough—a new ten-speed bike to ride to church, more time to enjoy the other gifts. I declined my son's request. That I'd do again; the mistake I made was one of approach. Later I was to overhear the lad complain to his mother, "You can't talk to him. He never listens."

To a man who thinks of himself as ideally suited to

practicing nondirective counseling, the wound of that evaluative comment was gizzard-deep. I wanted to spring to my defense: "How can you say that? Is it my fault that you're always on the run and never have time to talk?" Thank God, I didn't. The lecture I might have given would have been just one more evidence of nonlistening.

In every human there is a basic instinct of self-defense. We naturally tend to protect whatever is a part of us and to take on at least enough aggressiveness to inhibit continued attack. Those of us who are ordinarily nonaggressive often give a more violent defensive response because we have to stir up enough reactive energy to act contrary to our natural temperament.

More forceful defensiveness also tends to result from attacks on our most vulnerable spots. Thus it often happens that things our children say and do put us on the defensive. Instead of dealing calmly with the words or action as an expression of how the child feels, we spontaneously retort with a too logical argument against what has been said or done. We cite incidents from the past to "prove" that the charge of favoritism (or "what haven't you") is unwarranted. We give many self-evident reasons to back up our point of view.

THE CHINK IN OUR DEFENSE

These defensive tendencies often do us great harm. To understand why this is so, let's look at what I felt like saying to my son on that Christmas Eve. What were the elements of my case for the defense?

First, denial of the charge. "How can you say that?" implicitly contains a plea of *not guilty*. This first point, common to most parental defenses, finds a range of expression from an innocuous, "I don't think so" to an impassioned, "After all I've done for you!"

Second, counteraccusation. "You're always on the run
and never have time to talk" pushes the finger of blame in
the opposite direction. Sometimes the counteraccusation
ignores the original charge and points to some unrelated
fault in the accuser: "Look who's talking. If you'd do the
chores you're supposed to, we'd get along a lot better."

Often our case for the defense would be worthy of the
world's greatest criminal lawyers. And the devastating
effect on the parent-child relationship would do credit to the
world's greatest criminals. Especially scathing is the effect
on the parent himself.

Unfortunately, once a child begins to succeed regularly
in putting his parent on the defensive, he finds it a very
satisfying kind of game. By taking an offensive position, the
child avoids threat to his own ego, thus making potentially
unpleasant experiences easier for him to handle. For the
parent, though, these disagreements take a heavy toll.

Every power struggle with our children makes it more
difficult to react positively to future disagreements. Each
time a parent enters such a struggle with a child, it makes
self-acceptance more difficult. Losing the struggle increases insecurity; winning brings feelings of guilt. In
either situation, the parent's self-esteem is lessened, and he
or she is inclined to be even more defensive in the future.

The heart of the problem—the real chink in our
armor—is the *childishness* of these attempts to establish our
own adequacy. We need to grow beyond the "not me—look
at you" stage. To be ready to admit our shortcomings is a
prerequisite to proud parenthood.

ACCEPTING OURSELVES

If we are to reach this goal, we must begin by accepting
ourselves. We cannot experience pride in parenting if we
reject the real persons we are. We must be willing to plunge

ourselves freely and wholeheartedly into family living *exactly* as we are.

True self-acceptance requires that we know ourselves. If we see only shadows of our true selves—those behaviors that show our good side—this is not really accepting the fullness of what we are. Imagining a perfect conformity between ideal self and true self makes it very easy to like what we think we are and to accept it completely. But we deceive ourselves.

We all engage in some deception of this kind. We hide our worst qualities from ourselves because we fear that a revelation of our true natures would be unbearable to us and unacceptable to our associates. We are subtly dishonest about the habits, actions, and thoughts that do not fit the ideal image we have of ourselves. Unconsciously, we try to avoid facing our true selves because we are afraid of discovering things we don't like.

A father was walking through a cemetery with his son. As they talked of life and death, they drank in the peaceful atmosphere that surrounded them. From time to time they would pause and read one of the glowing epitaphs inscribed on the headstones.

As they reached the end of their tour and the father read one last inscription out loud, his young son turned inquiringly to him and said, "Gee, Dad, where are all the bad people buried?"

We bury the bad people we are deep inside ourselves. We really don't want to know persons so different from the ideal images we have created for ourselves.

But it is precisely that other person in us, our true self, that we must make welcome. We must cease being strangers to ourselves. The depth of our self-knowledge determines how we handle different situations, how we react to others, and how we want to be treated. The extent

to which we can accept our true selves will determine how
fully we can accept our children.

OUR TRUE FEELINGS

Our feelings are an important part of what we are.
Chapter 5 dealt with the importance of recognizing our true
feelings, admitting them outright, and finding constructive
outlets for them. Our main concern in chapter 5 was anger.
But there are numerous other emotions that stir within us.
There are countless hidden corners of our temperament
and personality. It's important that we remain open to
discovering any and all aspects of our real selves.

Most of us have barely survived the agonies of adolescence ourselves when we venture into the world of
parenthood. The turbulence has scarcely quieted. Still
smoldering within us are the remains of an inferno of
confused, angry feelings.

Then there comes into our lives an infant, "mewling and
puking" as Shakespeare says. And the crying—the screaming! How it wears on tired nerves! The impulse can be
strong to smother cries and crier with a pillow. The rage of
the child brings forth a similar emotion, proportionate in its
intensity. The urge to hit, to shake, even to pick up and hurl
across the room!

These are not sick feelings. They are not feelings to be
ashamed of. They are feelings to admit and accept, to deal
with as constructively as we can under the circumstances.

Such feelings will continue to be present as your child
grows up. His toddling will cause inconvenience when you
can least afford it. Seemingly incessant demands for your
attention will make you want to scream out a plea to be left
alone for a while. The new problems that lurk behind the
school doors will seriously threaten your sense of adequacy.
As you see your child growing away from you, you will often

feel that you have failed. You will see yourself losing control over his life. You will resent his moves toward independence.

Emotions that intrude on parent-child relationships are a universal experience. Every parent, from time to time, feels inadequate and then tries to appear omnipotent. Or he may experience hurt, and feel impelled to get even.

Our negative emotions can serve the same useful purpose as physical pain. Recurring chest pains warn me that something is awry in my physical condition. I seek medical attention that will enable me to take care of the problem and live a longer, happier life. Emotional upset can serve a similar diagnostic purpose. Feeling extreme frustration as I try to help my son understand a math problem, I ask myself why it's so important to me to be able to communicate effectively. The self-ideal of the perfect teacher is an icon that I must dethrone. Then I am able to accept myself more completely and be more helpful to my son.

Every day you are knee-deep in opportunities to start moving toward a richer, fuller life as a parent. Start by being honest with yourself. Admitting your limitations and self-doubts is half the battle. Let yourself be real; don't close your eyes or mind to actuality.

ARE YOU UNREAL?

Many of us have lost touch with ourselves. We suffer from a sense of personal unrealness. We have no true awareness of what we feel or what motivates us to act in certain ways. As a result, we remain enslaved by specters from the past, and we relinquish our freedom to live life in its fullness in the present.

Some parents teach children to detach themselves from their emotional experiences. A young lad falls on the sidewalk and begins to cry over his scuffed knee. Dad says emphatically, "Big boys don't cry." A girl sees an attractive skirt in the window, and Mother, noticing the repulsive price tag, says, "You don't really want that."

A doctor gave a five-year-old a shot and then said, "There now, that didn't hurt, did it?"

She looked angrily at him and replied, "You mean you've never had that done to you?"

Thus the child learns to disown his feelings and to become unaware of what emotions rise up within himself. He develops numerous techniques for warding off his feelings, barricading himself behind walls of muscular and other physiological tension. Protecting himself from his feelings becomes reflexive, so that each time he is threatened by a feeling he does not wish to experience, he erects the same kind of defense.

But it's not all the parents' fault. Every young life contains within it many experiences that stir up painful emotions. When these feelings become too severe, it is natural for the young person to seek escape through a denial of his feelings.

Naturally enough, then, most people grow to adulthood carrying a burden of much unacknowledged pain. Large areas of the past experiences that have brought us to be what we are have been blotted from our awareness. The repression of significant feelings and memories keeps us from much crucial data about ourselves. We fail to understand why certain events cause us to react in strange ways. Our overreaction to things our spouse or children do remains a mystery.

SELF-CONCEALMENT

Unfortunately, we often stoutly protect ourselves from exploring those hidden areas of our past. Subconsciously, we maintain our defenses and guard against confronting past pain that we have never permitted ourselves to acknowledge. Almost inevitably, we distort and rationalize rather than realistically confront conditions that have brought us to the present situations in our lives.

Thus we reach the point of alienation from our true selves. Self-alienation arrests our growth as persons. My real self is able to grow only when I stop repressing it and allow it just to be. Self-alienation keeps me from moving toward the goal of a healthy personality.

Self-alienation also keeps me from moving toward love. If I cannot be myself, not let myself be known truthfully and fully, then I can never love or be loved. Loving requires knowledge of the person who is loved. How can someone love me if he doesn't know me? How can I love one whom I do not know?

Self-awareness is also related to physical health. If I am trying to protect aspects of myself from being known—by me or by others—I will be under frequent or constant stress in my attempt to hide my true self. The very presence of other people might serve to evoke anxiety, heightened muscle tension, and other physical reactions to stress.

Doctors are discovering increasing evidence that asthma, colitis, ulcers, and migraine headaches are often the products of repressed emotions and needs. The majority of our repressive tendencies stem from our unwillingness to let our real selves be known.

The problem is especially acute with men. Women are much more able to disclose themselves. Men are driven much more to assume unreal roles. Dr. Sidney Jourard hypothesizes that there may be a connection between men's difficulty in self-disclosure and their shorter life expectancy. He suggests that "being manly" may be slow suicide.

For example, fathers need to get rid of the belief that

demonstrations of warm feeling are either effeminate or undignified. We often need to be convinced that it takes a real he-man to exhibit genuine human tenderness without feeling threat to the male self-image.

How does self-deception sound? Perhaps you occasionally hear yourself saying something like this:

"Those can't possibly be my real feelings."

"That wasn't really me saying that."

"I know this is stupid, but . . ."

"Now what would cause a person to feel that way?"

Sometimes, as soon as we begin to be aware of our true feelings, we abort the process and quickly convince ourselves that we are mistaken. Again, we might refer to some action as belonging to an inferior order of reality, saying in effect that that behavior doesn't count. Sometimes we use self-insult to put distance between ourselves and our feelings. Or we might use impersonality to protect ourselves from awareness that certain emotions are really ours.

SELF-HATE

Many people are strongly inclined to hate themselves. They have an image of what they should be, but they see themselves as falling woefully short of this ideal. At times their hatred and contempt for themselves are plainly visible as moods of depression. At other times, though, the self-contempt is more hidden, perhaps behind a mask of indifference or arrogance.

One's self-hate almost never has any relationship to whether such feelings are deserved. Many talented persons, many who have numerous interpersonal skills, suffer from extreme self-hate, often because of unconscious guilt.

You've probably known persons covering the whole range from self-hate to self-esteem. Some women are so in need of ego-building that they seize even the smallest compliment and drain it completely. If the butcher winks at such a woman and says, "That's sure a pretty dress you have on," he can be sure of being quoted to the next two dozen people she passes in the aisle. And while she's at it, the lady will probably throw in a few choice items about how smart her kids are or about her husband's promotion (ten years ago?).

Persons who have not developed normal emotional security may need constant assurance of being accepted or loved. They cannot recognize adult ways in which love may be shown to them, such as recognition or respect. Rather, they need frequent physical, verbal, or material displays of acceptance. Others are so lacking in security that even though love is shown to them, they are never satisfied. They need so much reassurance that no amount of loving expression can fill the need.

Enjoying expressions of love and acceptance is not immature, of course. Mature persons, though, will not crave them constantly or feel crushed or furious when they are not forthcoming.

A more self-accepting woman doesn't need the comfort of compliments quite so much. She may even develop considerable skill at self-effacement. If you say, "Your daughter is the best looking youngster on the block," she might say, "Thank you. Takes after her father in almost everything." If you say, "I just love that painting," she'll reply, "Woolworth special—$3.98."

ESCAPE

One who is self-acceptant can also face up to failure. Of course, accepting one's failures is never easy. It's a lot more pleasant to blame the other guy. Or we can just close our minds.

Two hobos were sitting on a riverbank. One of them began to express his true feelings about their profession.

"You know," he said, "being a tramp ain't what it's cracked up to be. I'm tired of nights on park benches and wondering where I'll get my next meal. Nobody wants you. Everybody looks down on you." He sighed.

His companion replied, "Well, if that's the way you feel about it, why don't you get yourself a job?"

The first hobo sat straight up and stared in amazement. "What!" he exclaimed. "And admit I'm a failure?"

We all fail sometimes. And these failures inevitably make us less acceptable to ourselves. But we ourselves aren't failures until we stop using our unsuccessful experiences as growth opportunities.

We use countless ways to try to escape from our real selves. Some people move aimlessly from city to city or from job to job. Sometimes we physically separate ourselves from the people and places that would lead to self-knowledge, taking refuge in a hubbub of activities for good causes, in the compulsion to shave strokes off our golf score, or in the crowded solitude of the neighborhood bar.

Some of us use mental escape. Although our bodies continue to go through the motions of living our lives, we let our minds run off to more attractive, safer places and times.

Of course, this running away solves nothing. The real situation remains. We take with us our memory, our recorded emotional experiences, our selves—everything that has brought us to where we are.

TOWARD SELF-KNOWLEDGE

To get to know ourselves, we need to deal with this drive to escape. We need to try to approach the content of our inner experience as a noncritical observer. We need to come as one who is interested in noting and describing facts, not in pronouncing moral judgments. We need to approach ourselves with the conviction that knowing ourselves as well as we can is worth the agony that it often entails, simply because it is a necessary first step to becoming what we want to be.

For many years, one aspect of my own life that I was unable to accept was my lack of success as an athlete. In the world of physical competition that surrounds the growing boy, my ineptness at sports cost me a great deal in peer esteem and feelings of self-worth. Even in basketball, the one sport in which I was able to develop some amount of skill, my many hours of practice failed to make me proficient enough to offset my lack of coordination.

Throughout my youth, I had repeated fantasies about being a great basketball player. As the years slipped by me, though, I began to see that I could never attain this ambition.

Then one day I woke up and discovered that I was the father of six boys. The fantasies of my youth came alive again, and I began to envision my sons in jerseys and trunks—a complete team, with one very capable "sub" ready to enter the game at any crucial moment.

Unfortunately, "like father, like son" turned out to be more fact than fiction. Only one of the half-dozen showed any inclination toward basketball, and he has always been six inches shorter than the second smallest kid in the class.

My own lack of success has given me considerable empathy for my sons as they have struggled to make it in the young sports world with very limited skills. I can appreciate how the boy feels who wants very much to get on the football team, but more often finds the football team on him. I know the feelings of the lad who tries out for track and discovers that the problem is not that the other boys on the team look *down* on him but that they look *back* on him.

That's the positive side. On the other hand, tinges of personal regret still creep up from time to time, and I realize that I'm still in the process of accepting my own limitations.

TASK OF A LIFETIME

At each stage of our lives, the process of struggling with ourselves brings fulfillment. As we evaluate our conduct and try to find ways of handling our emotional reactions and psychological needs, we are helping ourselves as well as our children. In our attempts to guide our children, we must inevitably deal with our own conflicts, thereby achieving a new level of maturity.

Nevertheless, self-acceptance remains a lifetime job. If we keep an open mind and a reasonably objective view, we learn continuously about ourselves. In the process we discover some of the personal characteristics we have repressed from our awareness. Each time we recognize a personal deficiency, we reconfirm our self-acceptance. Then we can renew our efforts to improve.

How we see ourselves is directly related to what we think life is all about. We see ourselves in relation to our world, and this relationship may be friendly or hostile. For the most part, our basic ideas about this relationship are formed early in life, and without conscious effort, they remain unrevised as we grow older. Gaining more experience, we tend to interpret the things that happen as confirming our self-image. Instead of reexamining our first impressions, we seek ways of substantiating them.

A child who feels, for example, that the world is unkind to him is likely to experience this unkindness throughout his life. He might seek out people who are likely to hurt him, never being conscious of his basis for selecting friends and associates. He might perform acts that bring him punishment, or simply imagine that he is being hurt by people who aren't mistreating him at all.

"He started it!" said the little guy who was being reprimanded for biting the doctor. "He hit me on the knee with a sledge hammer!"

As adults, we sometimes find ourselves worrying unrealistically. We may worry about what could happen, although the odds may be very much against such an occurrence. We even cause unlikely events to happen. Perhaps an auto accident in our youth caused us to be criticized severely for carelessness. If we believed ourselves to be without fault, the criticism may not have been rationally accepted at the time, but the hurt of the criticism may have remained. Now, feeling guilty about unexpressed emotions, we may unconsciously seek events that fulfill the expectation of carelessness that has been impressed on us.

One mother, a desperate worrier, accepted some tranquilizers from her physician. "These will help you stop worrying so much about your son," he told her.

A month later she came back for a progress check. "How's Freddie?" the doctor asked.

"Who cares?" she answered.

WHAT ACCEPTANCE LOOKS LIKE

Six-year-old Bobby is a very shy child. Many children need encouragement; Bobby needs an entire cheering section. Today he comes in crying, "That new kid up the street took my G.I. Joe!"

Mother has seen the new kid up the street. He's several inches smaller than Bobby and doesn't look nearly as strong. Memories of being pushed around crowd in on Mother. The anger she felt as a child but never dared to express swells in her now. She hates Bobby's weakness and almost hates him for it.

Then she remembers. All these feelings are as much a part of her real self as the haunting memories from the past. Willing firmly to accept herself and her child, she swallows the "Take it back!" that almost slips out, and she says instead, "It hurts to have him take your things, doesn't it?" We don't like it when somebody pushes us around, but sometimes we just can't bring ourselves to fight back."

Bobby will probably be surprised at his mother's response, especially if she has been less acceptant in the past. But he'll feel better that his mother knows how he feels and doesn't reject him for it. In time, he will be able to look more objectively at his emotions and possibly begin to realize that he can overcome his lack of courage.

Accepting ourselves is letting ourselves be fully aware of feelings, thoughts, desires, and actions. We give up denying our emotions, and begin to acknowledge them as our own. We don't place moral judgment on our feelings, thoughts, or actions. We come simply with a desire to be aware, and we suspend our moral judgment until we have objectively accepted what we are.

First, get rid of the idea that you must be perfect. This isn't an all-or-none process. We need to lay aside our standards of perfectionism, even though we'll unconsciously pick them up again from time to time. Go on reminding yourself that nobody is perfect and that no one expects it of you.

Then proceed to let yourself get involved as honestly as possible with other people. You might find a trustworthy friend with whom you can honestly and openly share yourself. By deeply sharing your fears and hopes with people you can trust, you will let yourself come out from your hiding places and become known.

Third, begin to act like the kind of person you want to

become. If you would like to be a parent who has excellent rapport with his children, begin to talk with them as if it were natural and easy for you to communicate openly. If you find yourself wishing that people liked you better, find opportunities to act like a popular person. This is not dishonesty or hypocrisy; an important part of the becoming process is to lead yourself in the direction you want to go.

STEP BY STEP

Let's look again at that three-step process. Getting rid of our perfectionism will make us more open to self-discovery. We need to be ready to recognize both the good and the evil that are in us. To know only one or the other, only the good or only the evil, is not to know the real person.

This does not mean that we should spend countless hours searching out our faults and limitations. Too much searching merely distorts what we are looking at. By a law of its own nature, self looks at self through an imperfect lens. In his mercy, our Creator hides many of our faults—from us and from himself.

Self-discovery comes rather from considering him in whose likeness we are made. We can contemplate God as we know him through faith. And we can deepen our knowledge of him and of ourselves by interacting openly with other people. This is the second step in the process of self-acceptance.

Let your real self be revealed, then, in your relationships with those around you. Let the experiences and conversations that you share with them illuminate the dark corners of your soul. Try for the openness to admit your shortcomings, at least to yourself, when they become obvious.

The third step is acting like what you want to become. As you take this step, you'll need to be patient; you may have

some trouble adopting your new role. Don't give up, for
example, if you find it difficult to come up with the right
way of saying things. Remember, Noah Webster spent
thirty-six years finding the right words.

SELF-LOVE

Acting like the person you want to become will make you
more lovable to yourself. Self-love is essential if we are to
love others. The parent who does not love himself is
incapable of loving his children. He might be able to *adore*
them; adoring is making someone big and ourselves little.
Or the parent's sense of personal incompleteness may lead
to possessiveness of the children, which is often mistaken
for love. Real loving, however, depends upon conditions
within oneself that make it possible to accept human
nature. If you don't have love, you can't give it.

We need to rid ourselves of the false notion that love for
others and love for ourselves are mutually exclusive. Just as
it is virtuous to love one's fellowman, so also it is a good
thing to love oneself, since you are a human being too.
"Love thy neighbor as thyself" implies respect for one's own
integrity and uniqueness as a foundation for love and
respect of others.

It's important to realize that selfishness and self-love are
opposites. The selfish person is a taker. He wants
everything for himself and feels no pleasure in giving. He
judges everything outside himself in terms of its usefulness
to him. But all of this concentration on self derives from
loving himself too little. His lack of self-acceptance leaves
him empty and frustrated. He makes an unsuccessful
attempt to compensate for his lack of self-love by possessiveness and extreme self-concern.

Again, the process of acquiring self-love is never really

finished. As much as we would like to succeed at complete self-acceptance, this goal can never be realized in this life. But in trying, we move toward that kind of satisfaction that caused one husband to boast that he had won the battle with the computer of life. He was spindled and mutilated, but he didn't fold.

CHAPTER 7

UNSURE OF DECISIONS?
USE YOUR CONSULTANT

GIVING IN

For some parents it's very difficult to stand firmly behind the decisions they make. When faced with opposition from their children, they tend to back down—or they give in by not requiring the kids to carry out their obligations.

If you find that you sometimes have this problem, imagine with me for a minute. You are a business executive. Completely on your own, you must decide how to invest six million dollars of a company's assets. You know only a little about investments, and you don't have time to learn more.

The decision would be very difficult, wouldn't it? And once you had decided, it would probably be easy for someone to talk you into changing your mind. In fact, you'd be likely to give in almost as readily as you sometimes do to your children.

Now how does that happen? What takes place when you yield to your children, even though you know you should stand firm? Well, suppose you've issued a command of some kind. Your son or daughter is playing the familiar deaf role. A sphinx would show as much acknowledgment. Maybe you repeat the order two or two dozen times. Then, rather than engaging in a major conflict, you decide— accurately—that it would be easier to forget the whole thing.

THE PRICE YOU PAY

But this act of surrender takes its psychological toll on both your child and you. The young person, aware of your vulnerability, is less likely to exert himself in the future, and this weakness will be damaging. Similarly, you will either feel guilty about your own weakness or rationalize it. As a result, you will continually become more insecure.

A sense of failure on the part of the parent will often result in strong feelings of inadequacy. This outlook is self-perpetuating. The more inadequate the parent feels, the more discouraged he becomes. The more pessimistic his outlook, the more likely he is to make serious mistakes in his relationships with his children.

One of the greatest problems springing from this sense of inadequacy is indecision or grave inconsistency in the parent's reaction. The parent who has no real plan or purpose in his dealings with his children is likely to go from extremes of severity to overindulgence. At one time he will beat the child for a given kind of behavior, and then, regretting his action, he is likely to try to make up for it through exaggerated displays of affection.

Often such a parent reacts to his inability to deal with his children by saying, "I've tried everything. I don't know what to do next." True, he has tried everything, but he has given nothing a fair trial. Lacking the confidence to pursue a given, definite line of action, he moves from one course to another and uses his puzzlement as an excuse to dodge his real responsibility.

Recognize, then, that insecurity about the decisions you make is the reason you find yourself giving in or yielding to resistance. This insecurity may be partly or totally unconscious, but it undermines your conscious efforts to be more firm. In varying situations it may take the form of fear that your commands or expectations may turn out to be—

    a. unenforceable—you fear that if you fight willfully to have the command obeyed, your child will outmaneuver you, and you will lose face in defeat;

    b. unreasonable—you fear that an argument over the logic of your expectation will cost you a loss of face for the same reason;

    c. inconsistent—you fear that enforcing a command or expectation would compel you to deal with some personal problem or trait you can't handle ("practice what you preach").

USE YOUR CONSULTANT

So, what can you do about this insecurity? Just remember your investment decision. In our make-believe situation you had little knowledge and no opportunity to increase your knowledge. In real life we often behave as if the same conditions exist. We make quick decisions about what our children should or may do. Under the pressure of getting a job done, we fail to consider what the children's reaction might be, or how things will appear from their perspective. Even when we do try to take their feelings into account, we usually project inaccurately.

As in the investment situation, we really have little knowledge. We don't know how our children see things. We're not sure how they will react.

But we can find out. Seldom do we really have to make the decision with this limited information. Most often we can take time to discuss the need or the situation with the person who can best enlighten us.

Rational dialogue with our children offers the best available insurance against eventually backing down. We need to learn to defer decisions until we can get more information. Ask the child for his opinion. Approach him rationally, with as little emotion as possible. Be willing to discuss, but never to argue.

Getting a child's feelings about a prospective order or rule need not take much time. A statement such as, "I'd like you to let me know where you're going whenever you leave the house after dark" conveys the parent's wish and invites the child to react. He will probably give his appraisal of the suggestion in a few words, and the parent can then decide whether to make it a rule of operation.

"How would you feel about taking over the grass-cutting duties this summer?" This question will either obtain a child's commitment to the assignment or give him an opportunity to express opposition. If his negative feelings are strong, the parent may decide to let him choose some other regular chore.

Occasionally, of course, it will be difficult to reach agreement. Sometimes the amount of dialogue required may exceed the time available. If the decision cannot be deferred longer, the parent will have to exercise his best judgment at that time. Whatever the decision, the child will feel better for having been asked his opinion.

COMMUNICATING DECISIONS

After the dialogue has taken place, the parent must make a firm decision. Then he must communicate this decision, along with any necessary instructions, to the child. We often assume that the child will infer our commands from what we say. Explicit, simple directions are seldom out of line.

Ideally, such information-providing dialogue is a continuous process, so that we obtain our children's viewpoints spontaneously. But as a temporary means of instituting continuous dialogue, why not take a few minutes to ask your child's opinion on the next several noncritical job assignments you plan to make? Your investment in the parent-child relationship is worth much more than six million dollars!

WHAT'S REALLY IMPORTANT?

Getting the child's viewpoint before making decisions that affect him or her is one way to avoid backing down. But there are also many decisions that you can relieve yourself of completely by turning the responsibility over to your child. You'll have to consider the age of your child and the importance of the decision to be made.

Ellen's father had reached the point of desperation. The six-year-old had been sitting and looking at a full plate since the beginning of the meal. Finally, her exasperated father said, "Child, why don't you eat? You don't like vegetables, you don't like salad, and you don't like meat. What do you like?"

Ellen eyed her father for a moment and then replied demurely, "Why, I like you, Daddy!"

Through a miraculous gift of nature, some young girls know how to wrap fathers around little fingers. One strongly positive aspect of this talent is that it keeps relatively unimportant things from getting all out of perspective.

From time to time, all parents need to be reminded of what things are really important. Otherwise, we'd wear ourselves out mountain-climbing over molehills. Every parent sometimes has to act blind and deaf. We need to overlook a few insignificant happenings and to deal mildly with many relatively unimportant matters. Then when we really need to react strongly concerning something important, for example, a serious disciplinary matter, our children will realize the seriousness of the situation. They will not be confused at having been scolded for various things that have little significance.

POSSIBLE REACTIONS

Let's look in again on the coy little dear who won't eat. Although Ellen has her father where she wants him, her mother is not so easily victimized. After all, it takes a lot of time and energy to put an attractive meal together every day. To have Ellen just sit and stare into her far-off land of dreams is insulting. Mother feels compelled to say something. Now which of the following reactions might be effective?

a. "Here, open your mouth," Mother says, shoveling up a half-dozen of those delicious fresh peas. "You're going to eat this food if I have to stuff it down your throat."

b. "Tell me about your day at the office, Dear," she says to her husband, ignoring Ellen completely. Meanwhile she thinks, "I refuse to let this kid get me down. If she wants to starve herself to death, the hell with her."

c. "We'll have dessert in about five minutes," Mother announces to the entire family. Then, with a glow of pride, she adds, "I made peach cobbler today." As always, the rule applies that dessert goes with a clean plate.

d. All of the above.

Answer: d. Each reaction has a chance of being somewhat effective. But the effects are likely to be different. Throat-stuffing might get the peas down, and if Ellen doesn't gag too badly, she might clear the rest of the plate and enjoy the cobbler. She'd also enjoy the lovely shades of crimson in Mother's complexion. She might even get a second helping of cobbler when Mother found her own appetite gone. (Or Ellen might never again be able to look at green vegetables without nausea.)

Ignoring might keep Mother from being aware of how upset she is. Mother and child would be spared the wrestling match, and while repressed emotion is tearing vigorously at Mom's insides, Ellen might begin to nibble on something nutritious. (Or Ellen might get the message, "The hell with her.")

Dealing with the situation in a matter-of-fact way maintains perspective. Ellen's decision to eat or not to eat is respected as a reasonably important free choice. If she decides negatively, she will survive until breakfast—without the cobbler. Mother can go on feeling good about the sumptuous dessert she's prepared for the family. She has made well-balanced nutrition *available,* and that should be a rather important value.

OPTIONING

Turning decisions over to children requires a certain amount of skill. It's not as easy as, "That's up to you." I'd like to offer a few words on the how-to of this important process. To have something to call it, let's give it the name *optioning.*

First, let me establish that besides helping the parent, this process is also good for the child. Optioning increases the child's sense of responsibility by giving him experience in making decisions for himself. As he gains confidence in his ability to choose wisely—and as he learns from his mistakes—the child's independent initiative gradually increases.

Basically, optioning is offering two or more clear alternatives from which the child makes an independent choice. Depending on what kind of decision it is, you might have to do one or more of the following:

a. Develop or clarify the available alternatives
b. Make sure the child understands that the decision is his to make
c. Increase his understanding of the probable consequences of each alternative

EXAMPLE

Take the case of Ida Idle, fourteen, who always puts off her chores. Ida is getting ready for a party. Noticing her wrinkled shirt, Mother realizes that Ida hasn't done her ironing for the week.

"Looks like you didn't get around to your ironing," her mother says.

Ida looks down at the front of her shirt and smooths it with her hand. "I haven't had time." she says.

Now this is a gal who spends more time on the phone than a switchboard operator at Bell Telephone. But she hasn't had time to do her ironing!

At a time like this, almost any mother would feel like shouting, "If you'd spend less time on the phone, you'd have time for a lot of things! You've got to get the lead out and start doing some work around this place!"

On the other hand, a softhearted mother might accept Ida's alibi and do the ironing herself. This really is a lot less painful than all the nagging and arguing.

Not Mrs. Idle. She nods agreement. "It has been a busy week, hasn't it?" she says. "But I think you still have time to run an iron over your shirt if you'd like. You'll probably be more comfortable at the party."

Mrs. Idle clarifies alternatives with "You still have time," establishes decision responsibility with "if you'd like," and presents probable consequences with her final statement. This is optioning.

BENEFITS

Ordinarily, optioning is more helpful than an angry response. Mother's shouting, in fact, may be just the reward Ida is seeking. There is usually a strong urge for parents to exert continued pressure in the hope that this will speed up task accomplishment. It seldom does. If (somehow) asserting pressure on a child does attain an immediate goal, there is more long-range damage done because we have reinforced his dependence on parent stimulus for carrying out an essential task.

Giving in doesn't help much either. Doing the ironing for Ida would also increase her dependence. Soon she'd be so lazy they'd be reviewing her birth certificate to make sure she's alive.

But besides helping your child gain independence, optioning can do great things for you. Leaving reasonable decisions up to your child will relieve you of much unnecessary responsibility. Many concerned parents are burdened with the feeling that they are totally responsible for everything their children do. No wonder we feel that there just isn't enough of us to go around.

With reasonable alertness you'll find many opportunities to use optioning. Your own life will be less cluttered, and your child will be developing self-confidence and independence.

GUIDING THE CHILD

Whatever the age of your child, optioning requires that you be willing to let your child make some unwise choices and learn from his mistakes. When a child chooses to dawdle and arrive late for school, for example, his decision is accepted. If school or home standards indicate that this choice incurs some form of punishment, no "I told you so" message is conveyed to the child. It is important to remember that the goal of optioning is not specific to the situation, like getting ready for school on time. Rather, it is a more general (and thus more valuable) goal, namely, developing responsibility and independence.

For the child to be ready to move toward this independence, he must have a reasonable measure of personal security. But denying the insecure child the opportunity to make decisions merely intensifies his unsureness. Rather than waiting until the child is more secure, then, the best way to help such a child is through shared decisions or *guided optioning*. In this process the parent increasingly involves the child in decisions young people should make, gradually shifting responsibility for the final judgment to the child.

DECISION BOUNDARIES

There are, of course, some decisions that even the most secure child should not be left to make for himself. For instance, a fifteen-year-old would not be permitted to decide to stay home from school for a week. When a child seeks to make a decision that is beyond his realm, the parent must exercise authority and identify the right course of action. It's a good idea to try to explain why the young person may not make this particular decision. Then try to provide at least one opportunity for him to make a legitimate choice on some other matter.

Although the range of a child's decisions increases with age, there are a few decision areas that are best considered the parents' responsibility as long as the child is subject to parental authority. These decisions all fall within the broad framework of religiomoral standards. When a teen-ager challenges his parents' ethical or religious beliefs, his motivation is typically twofold. First, he is indicating a need to move out from under the protective mantle at least far enough to analyze the reasons for believing certain things. And secondly, he is seeking information. Usually, the young person is relieved to find that a parent's commitment to basic beliefs is strong enough to justify insisting on certain standards.

Insisting on reasonable standards is as important as giving the child freedom of choice. The point is, that standards become real for the child only as he freely accepts them as legitimate guides for his conduct.

The child faced with a decision that is beyond him may be in a predicament similar to the bridegroom who asked the minister about his fee in the presence of his bride. "Just pay me whatever you think it's worth" was the minister's reply.

NEED FOR VALUES

Much has been said and written about modern-day rejection of traditional value systems. Today more than ever before, it is vital that those things that are really good and worthwhile be preserved for posterity. Parents must return to basic, enduring values, and free their children of the conflicting confusion of many specific rules. Children must be taught to be inner-directed, rather than slaves of regulations. We must show them how to apply values to everyday living.

One of the most direct means to this end is to clarify just what our values are and to make sure that we are reflecting them in the way we live. Adults need to *discover* the values to which they are, in fact, devoting their lives, and *compare* these with those they believe most important. Making sure that their own lives generally conform to their true values, parents are then in a position to interpret these values to their children as they impose required discipline on their lives.

Often the values that govern important decisions can be identified jointly by family members. If parents develop their key values together and allow children some participation in this process, there will be greater overall commitment to the results.

You may find it helpful to seek the help of your spouse and children in writing down six to ten of the most important things you want in your family life. One of the kids might make a poster to display these values on the family bulletin board. This will keep them closer to the everyday awareness of the entire family. Rely on these values as you make rules for your family and attempt to gain the obedience of your children.

Your list won't include all your values, of course. For this reason you'll have to avoid giving the impression that all rules or expectations for your children's conduct will hinge on this list. Nor should the listing be unchangeable. You may want to review it with your family once a month or so at first, later perhaps twice a year.

Just as you'll have many values of your own that aren't listed, your children, too, will have other things that are important to them. You'll need to be aware of some of these other values as occasions arise to seek your child's cooperation. But the listing will help you to think more often of the key values you share. You'll be more able to regulate your reactions to various situations.

DIFFICULTIES

It's not easy to save our thunder and drama for the important occasions. The link between everyday incidents and our rational values is usually hard to establish. As a result, we don't always give proper attention to the things that are most important, while relatively insignificant events often bring forth the strongest emotional response. It takes a constant struggle to overcome mental myopia and see things in proper perspective. Perhaps parental vision will be clearer in the year 2020.

The really crucial thing is that we keep trying. It's very important that our children get some idea of how the things we believe in can govern our actions. In the process, doubts are bound to arise. Only a heartless tyrant could avoid occasionally wondering whether a certain disciplinary action was necessary, or a given decision prudent.

But doubt is different from abdicating responsibility. If parents do not persevere in bringing up their children according to their convictions and values, they are leaving the shaping of children's beliefs to a variety of other influences over which they have almost no control. The young person whose values are molded primarily by television and other mass media, for instance, is in pitiable condition.

Another difficulty all parents experience is maintaining open communication with their children. To involve your child in decisions, to turn them over to him, or even to explain the reasons for a decision you have made, you must be able to communicate openly.

OBSTACLES TO OPENNESS

It's never easy to keep a truly open relationship with children, especially as they reach adolescence. Oh, you'll meet a lot of people who want you to think they're highly successful at it. And maybe a few are—if you think of the .200 hitter who gets an occasional clutch single as successful.

It took me many years to realize it, but some of those who

talk most about open relationships are the most closed into their own worlds. Professing is not practicing.

Recognizing this, I don't stew long over the walls that inevitably arise between my teen-agers and me. I can try going over the wall, or, if it's too high, finding a way around it.

Not that it doesn't hurt when you first run headlong into one of those walls. I remember the day my son finally gathered enough courage to call a certain girl for a date. Her refusal was shattering. He went to his room and closed the door. I found myself standing outside the door, wanting to share his disappointment, to let him know that I was suffering with him. If only my feelings could flow through the door as freely as the amplified roar of rock from inside! I raised my hand to knock. I stopped. The closed door was forbidding—a sign of a need for privacy that a parent dare not violate.

I was disturbed by the barrier between us. A concrete slab could not have been more obstructive than that hollow birch door. But as I thought about the incident, I saw it in better perspective. I began to realize that some obstacles to openness with our children are inevitable.

A major part of the problem, of course, is basic to the nature of adolescence. Still unsure of his own identity, the young person cannot often afford to lay himself open to others. To be open is to let others see him as he is and risk rejection. Others may not like what he is, and that's all he has.

Keep in touch with the teen you've raised, even when the only thing you seem to have in common is need for the family car. If you don't see each other often enough to talk much, try "rapping paper." You may find it easier to express honest feelings in notes. He can read them as he stops at the kitchen table to refuel. Sometimes he'll even want to talk about what's been written.

It's important to be jubilantly aware of every time our adolescents lay part of their undisguised selves before us and we respond in kind. Celebrate! The feeling of pride that is rightfully yours at such a time is a creative emotion. It has the potential of leading the way to new successes. This is a noble pride, based on gratitude for a blessing received. It is essential to maintaining a sense of parental dignity.

Above all, rejoice in your successes. Cherish the moments of closeness: the embrace of a young child telling you how much he enjoys your stories, the excitement of the elementary-schooler describing his thrill at getting the highest grade in the class, the joy-laden wink of the teen who has just passed his driving test, the infectious delight of the bride-to-be on the day she accepts his proposal.

Whatever your most tender communications might be, they will be rewarding enough to justify all the effort you can give to openness. Be available when your children need you. And do your best to let them look into the real you, like the four-year-old who lifted the eyelid of her napping father one Sunday afternoon and announced proudly, "He's still in there!"

CHAPTER 8

LOOKING
THE OTHER WAY?
TRY LOOKING UP

IGNORE NOTHING ·

Through the last four chapters we've considered some of the opportunities we have to use our natural tendencies as strengths. The same personality traits that incline parents toward punishment, anger, defensiveness, and insecurity can also be converted to *helping* our children. Now let's talk about a fifth tendency many of us have.

It sometimes happens that we become so discouraged with our children, or so unsure of our ability to help them, that we simply ignore patterns of behavior that should concern us. It's easy to do—easier, even, than not listening to things our children try to tell us in other ways.

There's a rather simple way to solve this problem. But first, let's be sure we understand the problem.

Every act of misbehavior contains a message for Mom or Dad. When we ignore the misbehavior, the child is likely to perceive this as lack of concern or lack of love. Even if he is

not conscious of the message behind his action, he'll get a
return message to the effect that we really don't care.

There's a subtle but important difference between
overlooking and ignoring, as I use the terms. I believe
parents must overlook a great deal, that is, let many
incidents go by without taking any overt action. This is done
consciously after the parent has taken notice of the behavior
and judged its importance. Often the child will be aware
that the parent has observed and chosen not to react. On
the other hand, I believe that parents must try not to ignore
anything in the behavior of their child, if ignoring means
acting internally and externally as if the incident had never
occurred.

Timmy is an extremely mischievous lad. When his
parents go out for the evening, the most important
information they give the baby-sitter is, "The aspirin are in
the medicine cabinet." When they return, the sitter says,
"Don't apologize for being late. I wouldn't hurry to get
back to Timmy either!" Timmy's mother knows that many
of his devilish deeds are designed simply to get attention.
She tries hard not to miss much of what he does, but she
often does nothing about minor misdemeanors that are
clearly intended for her attention. She then tries to pay
attention when Timmy does something good, and she
saves her punitive actions for more serious forms of
misbehavior.

There's hope for Timmy. His mother is taking the trouble
to observe the things he does. And when the situation
warrants, she takes action.

The parent who consistently looks the other way when
his or her children behave in questionable or undesirable
ways is taking a great risk. Countless things take place in
the lives of our children that we cannot possibly be aware of.

Ignoring those that happen before our eyes may lead to almost complete *ignorance* about what's happening.

NONINVOLVEMENT

In some families, although both parents are physically present, one is so uninvolved in the business of child rearing that the situation isn't very different from a one-parent home. I'm not sure which way things are headed in our equal-rights era, but in my experience it's the father who often fails to get sufficiently involved in bringing up the children.

Admittedly, some fathers get more than their fair share of the child-rearing burden. One mother tucked her young son in for the night and said reassuringly, "Honey, if you need anything through the night, just call Mommy—and she'll send Daddy in."

But there are other fathers who consider the children strictly Mother's responsibility. Artfully, they avoid taking responsibility for things that go wrong in the family. They remain passive and detached while their family life crumbles around them. In their relationships with Mom and children, they may seem very easy to get along with. They never yell; all they want is peace.

Because such fathers do not take an active role in maintaining a positive and creative style of family life, they fail to carry out the mission of family leadership. By not getting involved, they put their children in danger of emotional starvation. Mother is forced to be a tyrant because the complete burden of family discipline falls on her shoulders.

A father who allows himself to lapse into such a state of indifference forfeits his claim to proud parenthood. We cannot both abdicate our responsibility and take pride in the job we do.

THE SOLUTION

If discouragement or doubt is jeopardizing your understanding of your child or your ability to be a good parent, it's
urgent that you *look up*. We all need a much deeper
appreciation of our aliveness. Most of us have not begun to
realize our true potential. We tend to believe that ordinary
people must indefinitely go on being ordinary. The extent to
which this is true depends upon our definition of ordinary.
Perhaps we need to recall that the real destiny of ordinary
man is to be absorbed in the infinity of God.

Look up, then, to the God who created you and called you
to parenthood. Know that with this calling goes the
continuous support you need to do a good job. No matter
how great the problems of parenthood might seem, God's
help is always with us.

It's important that we learn to take disappointment in
stride and to accept our everyday mistakes as part of the
growth process. Every mistake we make can help us learn
to be a better parent. God's providence converts our
mistakes—even our deliberate ones—into the means of
achieving greater good.

What he asks of us is faith. He wants us to believe in his
power to see us through every difficulty that springs up in
our path. He wants our complete confidence.

We profess a theoretical belief that God constantly
supports us with his help. Too often, though, we fail to turn
to him in specific situations. Either we are simply
unmindful of his infinite love and power, or we fail to see
them as relevant to a given situation. We may ask, "What
could God do for me at a time like this?" A more meaningful
question would be, "What would I like to ask him to do?"
Times without number, God has shown us that faith in him
can bring wisdom and power beyond human imagining to
even the most desperate situation.

THE GOOD THINGS

With an abiding faith in God, there is no room for discouragement. We rest assured that his support will enable us to be good parents.

Once you have reestablished your confidence in God's power, you need only to allow for its sustenance. Maintaining your confidence is very important. To do this, you need to let yourself begin to see the many positive aspects of the behavior of your child and yourself. Make a diligent effort each day to see some of the many things that both of you are doing right. Rejoice in your successes as a parent. Take note of the many things your children do to make your life more pleasant. Be grateful for the big, important things—and the small favors.

A six-year-old once told Art Linkletter that she made her mother's life easier by helping her change her baby brother.

"And how do you do that?" Linkletter asked.

"Carefully," she replied.

It's easy for us to overlook many of the good things our children do. Because we consider certain tasks to be their duty, we notice only when these things are undone or carried out unsatisfactorily. But performance of our duty is all our *Creator* expects of us—and the reward *he* gives us is eternal!

THE NEED TO ESCAPE

Recognizing the good things will increase our ability to stay with our responsibilities when the going gets rough. To respond faithfully to the duties that come with parenthood, we need to overcome the universal human tendency to escape from difficult situations. There is not one of us who from time to time doesn't need to get away from it all. But we surely don't need to escape from the problems of the moment nearly as often as we think we do.

Many of the feelings that stir up in us a need for escape are matters of habit. They stem from things that have happened to us in the past, often in the impressionable childhood years. Without being aware of it, we often extend our childhood reactions through adolescence and into our adult behavior patterns. As a result we behave in ways that are inconsistent with the reality that surrounds us in our adult lives. We fail to realize that our feelings and behavior represent a continued defensive reaction against threats that are no longer present.

Cora was a twenty-five-year-old mother of two. The insecure reactions that were habitual parts of her behavior were beginning to be reflected in the conduct of her children in their early school years. When Cora was small, her father would often come home intoxicated and administer cruel and severe beatings for relatively insignificant offenses. As Cora talked through her current situation in counseling, she began to realize that she was allowing her childhood behavior patterns to endure in her responses to her husband. Although Jack was a mild-mannered man, he had occasional moments of anger, at which time Cora found herself cringing in the same way she used to as a child. Her manifest fears were having an effect on her children, and they were sharing in her unwarranted insecurity.

How do we break out of these habitual patterns?

Basically, we need to leave the past alone. We resolve to live in the real present and give ourselves the freedom to use our resources in full, wholesome living. We need not try for dramatic change in the persons we are. Not only is it unnecessary to try to become a different person, it is also impossible. Overcoming our habitual negative reactions is simply a matter of activating our unused resources and potentialities.

This is sometimes more difficult than it ought to be. Even though we long for a richer life, we experience the friction of considerable self-resistance as we attempt to move in that direction. Often our apparent inability to reach out for the fulfilling joy of living is simply a refusal to risk the pain of potential disappointment. Rather than commit ourselves to work toward a goal and face the possibility of not succeeding, we resign ourselves to our current status and turn our backs on opportunities to help ourselves and our children.

YOUR RESOLUTION

We need a fresh resolution. Decide what kind of parent you want to be, and then take the first big step in that direction. Don't let yourself be haunted by past failures. There's no greater obstacle to carrying out a good resolution than fear of failure. After numerous unsuccessful attempts, we hesitate to try again. Everyone likes success. Lack of success can seriously hinder not only the formation of the resolution itself but also the implementation of the good intentions we accumulate.

Another obstacle is indifference. "I spent two thousand on psychotherapy," said one young woman, "and after a year I found out that my main problem is apathy. But who cares?" Often we simply lack the will to succeed.

But there are other reasons, too, for our good but fading resolutions. Two common reasons are lack of reflection and overeagerness.

How many resolutions have you broken simply because you didn't stop to think about what you were doing? Stimulated by some word, object, or motive, you moved quickly to action. Either you didn't realize at all that you were breaking the resolution, or you blocked such thoughts from your mind.

At other times, the resolutions you have made may have been so ambitious and unrealistic that carrying them through was simply impractical. The alcoholic who resolves never to touch another drop without somehow gaining support and finding other means to deal with his problems is not likely to be successful. This same difficulty can arise if we make many resolutions that would affect our lives simultaneously.

In general, then, we can make it easier to keep resolutions by forming fewer of them—with greater determination.

A little optimism would help, too. We might try following the example of the Little Leaguer who was whistling contentedly in right field when a man happened to stop by to watch. The gentleman asked the right fielder what the score was.

"Eighteen to nothing," the lad replied. "We're losing."

"Well," the man observed, "you sure don't look discouraged."

"No, why should we be discouraged?" the boy said. "We haven't been up to bat yet."

No matter how old your children are (or how old you feel), there will never be a better time than now to begin looking up. Take a short time-out and consider the many opportunities you have every day to start taking a more positive outlook. Let's look at a few examples.

PRESCHOOL

If you are a new parent, let your participation in creating human life be the beginning of a new era of creativity for you. Far from letting yourself go stale because of family obligations, let yourself grow even as your child grows. May no one ever have to voice for you or your child Oliver

Wendell Holmes's lament for those who "die with all their music in them."

Look on the young child's bottomless cup of curiosity as one of his richest endowments. Those wide eyes that you think should be as heavy as yours are agog with appreciation of the wonder of life. How many ways can you think of to capitalize on this awareness?

Seek opportunities to lighten the mood of some of the trying days that inevitably come. When you get the worst of it, make the best of it. Maintain a sense of humor like the husband who said to the baby-sitter, "Can't we stay out till after midnight tonight? It's New Year's Eve, and all the other parents are doing it."

As your child becomes more active, put aside your pet projects and personal preferences to show an interest in his adventures. You brought him into this wonderful world; let him show it to you—one weed or crawling creature at a time. Your attention will be the reward that encourages his mind to reach out to new frontiers.

THE SCHOOL YEARS

Steel your heart against jealousy when your kindergarten daughter tells you of her first boyfriend. You'll still get your share of love notes, and it'll be years before someone not-nearly-good-enough takes her away. Think of all the wet good-night kisses you'll get before then.

Stand outside with your child at night, and lift eyes and hearts to the skies. As the Milky Way becomes more than a chewy candy, you'll both expand your awareness of the magnificence of creation. You may need the benefit of this spiritual uplifting when you face tomorrow morning.

Imagine occasionally how difficult your children could make life for you if they really wanted to. Think of some of the bad things they *don't* do. And look for a positive side to some of the things that cause you vexation. "Why don't you ever talk about the dirt I track *out*?" the nine-year-old asked his mother.

Show some pride and confidence in your children as you discuss them with their teachers. Even if you're tempted to use an assumed name when you go to PTA meetings and teacher conferences, be sure to say something good about each child to each of his teachers. If you won't stick up for the rascals, who will?

Recognize the unprecedented awareness that characterizes today's youth. Never has a generation been more conscious of the problems and blessings of the entire world. If it often seems that your teen-ager's entire world is the area of the telephone and the refrigerator, don't be fooled. You can test his awareness by trying to do something you don't want him to know about.

Find something you can comment positively about in your daughter's boyfriend, even if the huge ball of hair with eyes peering through is not to your liking. If his deportment suggests that your daughter should major in wildlife management, how about noticing how strong he is or how well he plays the guitar. Oh, come now, there must be something!

SEE YOUR SUCCESSES

In addition to seeing the bright side of our children's behavior, we need to pay attention to our own accomplishments. This is often difficult. For some of us it takes constant effort just to avoid scraping our chin on the pavement when we walk.

I hope this book will help you realize how many things you're doing right for your children. I hope you'll feel somewhat like one mother who reviewed part of this book for me. She said she liked what she read because I was describing many of the things she does every day with her children. Seeing these techniques described in writing by a psychologist made her feel successful. I hope some of my suggestions seem so obvious to you that you wonder why I bother mentioning them. The mere fact that you're taking the trouble to read a book on parenting suggests that you are doing many things right. Not enough attention—yours or mine—is given to these successes.

Give a lot of thought to the things you usually do well. Step back and admire the attractive suit you sewed. Live again the class in which you were the top student, the successful meeting you conducted. Spend more time thinking about your accomplishments and less time regretting your mistakes.

It's important that the style of leadership you attempt to provide for your family is natural for you. The best parent you can become is one who uses well the talents and personal strengths you have.

The leadership a parent exerts, like the teamwork within the family, will depend for its style on the personalities of family members. A parent can exert rather strong leadership without saying a great deal or taking specific kinds of action. A mother's obvious enjoyment of dinner with the family—her interest in listening to the children talk about their day at school—is as important an assurance of family harmony as established guidelines for family conduct. Just by coming home after work because he likes his home, a father can contribute greatly to the future well-being of his children. Display of loving concern and modeling of good behavior are among parents' greatest gifts to their children.

It's almost impossible to overemphasize the importance of parental leadership in the home. Considerable research has pointed to the fact that the best adjusted children are those whose parents took a strong hand in guiding their development, exerting their authority in a firm but gentle way.

This leadership cannot be provided by a parent who withdraws from the family or turns his back on genuine, everyday living. We need to be with our children, observe their behavior and understand its meaning. We need to take the trouble to administer a touch of discipline when this is what a child needs—even if there's something else we'd rather be doing. We need to take time to give that small sign of affection until these sustaining acts become spontaneous. Above all, we need to renew our confidence in God so that we can bring ourselves to the state of mind reflected in a comment attributed to Pearl Bailey: "Life? I like to pour it out without measuring."

CHAPTER 9

OPEN YOUR HEART TO JOY

THE NEED FOR JOY

OK, I'm just rationalizing, but it really is more fun to have the family photographs in disarray on the closet shelf. Anytime I reach in and grab a handful, I can look forward to being surprised by a nostalgic reexperience of some treasured event—sometimes several.

And so the albums collect dust. Largely undisturbed are the snapshots from my childhood, held neatly in place by black mounting corners. In another volume are pictures of courtship days; these, too, are carefully mounted in order. Those were the days of orderly living, the often monotonous days before the walls of our home began to stretch outward like the precious womb in which our new life was joyously conceived.

The years go by so quickly! As the children arrive, the magic renews itself constantly because we can see the world through wondering young eyes. We find that we are surrounded by reasons to be joyful. Every parent's life is

117

filled with situations that touch the human heart and invite the song of joy to swell forth.

Look fondly into a child's eyes that have been lit from your own. Cradle in the crook of your arm a miniature reproduction of your own head. Smile into an infant face that has your mouth, your nose, or the most cherished features of your beloved.

Begin now to take time occasionally to study your young human's wondrous assets. Never be afraid to let your child catch you looking admiringly at him. If no one ever seems appreciative, his future experiences with mirrors are likely to be anything but pleasant.

It's important that we breathe freely of the joyous richness we have. Our hearts must be open, and this often requires conscious and continuing resolution. Rather than adopting the viewpoint of the cynic who defines parenthood as "a lottery in which you can't tear up the ticket if you lose," we need to see our role in life as the challenging opportunity that it really is.

Why is joy so important?

For one thing, the amount of joy we experience in our parenthood has a dramatic effect on our children. In fact, it influences everyone we come in contact with. Every day you issue, to your children and the others that share your life's experiences, numerous powerful invitations. Depending upon your enthusiasm and your appreciation for what you have, you invite your children to live or to die, to triumph or to surrender.

According to psychiatrist Sidney Jourard (*The Transparent Self*), we are constantly offering such invitations to those around us. When I am in your company, the way you make me feel causes me either to grow or to diminish. Similarly, I extend an invitation to you either to live or to die. By treasuring life in myself, I offer it to you. My life grows as I spend it. And as I open my heart to you, you experience some of my enthusiasm for living and loving, and you are drawn to share in my joy.

Share the fresh love of a little girl who skips lightly across the room, climbs up on a chair, and wraps her arms around my neck. Share the loyalty of a young son as he shadows his father, humming his own current through a toy electric shaver or a bright plastic lawn mower.

POSITIVE AND NEGATIVE

Unfortunately, the freshness of life passes away all too quickly for many of us. Too many parents end up over the hill without ever having climbed it. We set lofty goals for ourselves and our parenthood, but our journey toward the accomplishment of those goals has barely begun when we experience discouragement and defeat. The aspirations that once stirred us become lifeless. Our daily contact with our families degenerates into dreary monotony. We allow the joy of life to flee from us, leaving us with hollowness and boredom.

At a time like this, we need a new spark of inspiration. We need someone to remind us to look on the favorable side of things. I like, for example, the comment attributed to William Buckley that life can't be all bad when ten dollars will buy all the Beethoven sonatas and let you listen to them for ten years.

Some time ago, I was meeting with a group of teachers, and one of them asked me, "What is the most common cause of problems that kids have in school?" There are many possible answers to this question. Taking the approach of the profound philosopher who maintained that marriage is the chief cause of divorce, I might have answered, "Being born." Or, if I had been a bit more daring, I might have said, "Teachers." This answer would have allowed me to go on to talk about how teachers often inadvertantly contribute to classroom difficulties.

But I chose to give a different answer: "Parental negativism." Then I proceeded to explain that parents are often so overwhelmed by the problems of child rearing that they are unable to see the positive side of things. Eager to guide their children away from dangers to their physical and moral well-being, many parents fail to recognize the innumerable good things their children do. This tendency always to point up the negative aspects of children's behavior has a corroding influence on their self-respect and confidence.

On the other hand, being enjoyed is such a happy experience! When a parent focuses on the things he likes best about his child, it builds self-esteem. The parent's positive outlook develops in the child an appreciation for the good things in his or her life.

Life is full of beauty, and if we condition ourselves to recognize it, we will be richer as a result. Even life's most bitter experiences have a degree of beauty. I could give no better example of this than the parent who told me at the time of the death of her infant son, "I thank God for giving him to us for a little while. He did so much to brighten our lives."

Even in our darkest hour we may be able to force a smile and keep our gloom from invading the lives of those around us. If our children can be spared the agony of our most bitter moments, the "carefree existence of childhood" can be more a reality for them. Recognizing the power of a smile in influencing the attitude of others, we will be more ready to seek the brighter side of the unfortunate events of life.

This positive viewpoint is a way of living. You can't adopt it just by wanting to, but you *can* begin gradually to see things more positively by seeking specific occasions to look at the favorable side of things. In other words, you have a vocation to be an optimist.

Asked to write what an optimist is, one youngster put it this way: "When people go to see the optimist, they often find that their eyes and headaches have disappeared. And you never have to take off your clothes." Pick up a mirror and see your optimist today.

WATCH AND LISTEN

Cherish the beauty of each moment before it slips by to take its place in the mosaic of eternity. Open your senses to the innumerable simple joys that surround you every day of your life. Take time to appreciate the pleasure of walking along a quiet road or a wooded path beside a running stream. Appreciate the music of the laughter of children at play, of a bird's song, or of a distant church bell. Linger with a cup of coffee at the waking dawn, or hold your children close in the rich glow of a gorgeous sunset. There are so many simple joys in a parent's life!

In nearly every young child's face we see the same look—a look of expectation, trustfulness, and readiness to love. The dimples and the smile reflect a continuing joy, ready to burst forth at any moment in uncontrolled laughter. What could be more wonder-full than the face of a child? With each new discovery, there is the reflection of a mind searching for answers to what makes this go and why does this work this way.

And there the little one stands, his arms outstretched, his fist tightly clutching a freshly plucked bouquet of clover and dandelions.

For St. Patrick's Day, one Sunday school teacher asked her preschool children to bring to class "something green that you love." Most of the children showed up with their green dresses, books, or hats. But one young lad entered the classroom with an unusually big grin. Behind him in a fresh green dress was his four-year-old sister.

Your appreciation of the joyous things your children say and do will depend largely on your image of yourself. So will the pride you take in your parenthood. How you see yourself tends to set limits on your individual accomplishments. Your self-image tries to define what you can or cannot do.

If you are oriented to success, you are often mindful of past achievements. This awareness spurs you to expect continued success. Pride in your parental role comes naturally, and you find it easy to recognize the joys in your life.

On the other hand, if you are a failure type, you think constantly of mistakes you've made, and you expect to go on failing. Accept what you are and keep trying to look for the bright side. One parent of a ten-year-old ("He's going to be eleven—if I let him") said his child is a born doctor: he can't write anything that anyone can read.

If you watch and listen carefully, you may hear your children saying something like this:

"Gee, Mom, your hair smells really cool—just like french fries."

"Our baby's coming from an egg and a seed, so it's gonna look like a chicken with a flower in its mouth."

"If you don't eat, Johnny, you'll grow up to be a midget."

"Why doesn't God let the sun out at night when we need it most?"

"Why do I have to wash my hands? Dirt don't show on chocolate."

"Daddy, what color is a paternity suit?"

These bits of lightheartedness make it easier to put up with the aggravations we all experience: the unfinished do-it-yourself jobs, the dripping faucet, the screens that stay in all winter, the way you have to stretch your every joint to make the bunk beds, the puppy who acts as if you put the paper on the floor so he could read the want ads.

HOW WE RESPOND

The parent who sees the humorous side of the many wearying events that occur in every life is able to transmit this positive outlook to his children. Laughter in the midst of frustration is sometimes the only means of lifting the burden from our hearts. No one can escape the disappointment of unfulfilled expectations, of determined striving after a goal that leads only to a blind alley. But these dark moments are only temporary, and viewed in proper perspective, they can often be sources of genuine amusement.

How much better off we would be if we could accept the simple outlook of the clergyman who told his congregation, "Children, just love God and dance." Let's try to free our hearts to jump with joy at the presence of our loved ones and the happiness that our life today can bring us. When we shed our warped notions of how things should be and accept the reality of how they are, we will be more free to live and love.

Recognize that problems do not make happiness impossible. Instead, the action we take to solve our problems can bring about the personal growth and satisfaction that comprise much of the real joy of developing ourselves together with our children. As problems arise within the family, we can struggle together to solve them. This struggling will draw us closer.

Sometimes we'll blunder in the way we respond. This, too, we must learn to take in stride. Perhaps in the heat of emotion we speak without sufficient thought. Someone noted that there is one good thing about talking before you think: you find out what's really on your mind. Or perhaps our response is the type that gives the child reason to comment, "When I get mad at you it's temper, but when you get mad at me it's nerves." Well, we all have our bad days.

Fumbles were causing Oklahoma's undoing in a football game against Notre Dame. Each time Coach Bud Wilkinson's Oklahoma team got possession and tried to come back, someone would fumble again.

At half time, as the team stood on the steps waiting for the band to finish its show, the drum major threw his baton into the air—and dropped it! With this, a fan turned to Wilkinson and said, "I see you coach the band, too."

No matter how good our coaching has been, we all fumble many chances. Regretting opportunities we've missed or feeling guilty about our blunders is generally nonproductive. Why miss today's golden chances while you're fretting over an irrevocable yesterday?

Go on responding as supportively as you can to your child's expressions of need. Listen to the things he says, and let him know you understand. Notice the tear in the corner of his eye. Interpret his finger in his mouth as more than just a habit to be corrected. Know that when he comes hurrying to ask Dad a question and suddenly forgets it, he may simply want to be close for a while.

YOUR NATURAL STRENGTHS

Every one of us has things we do well. We need to build on these natural strengths.

Your strengths may be skills or talents you've worked hard to develop. They may be personality characteristics that have emerged with maturity. Or they may be simply a result of the role we find ourselves in.

Someone has said that it doesn't matter how irresponsible a man might seem. If you see his children standing with noses flattened against the window when he's due home for supper, you can trust that man with anything.

In cultivating our natural strengths, we need to make the most of the here and now. Too often we have a romantic, rosy vision of the past. The future, on the other hand, beckons to us as a better time ahead. Meanwhile, the present seems filled with problems, pains, and imperfection. But now is the only time we can act. Wishful thinking about the past or idle dreams of the future are nothing more than wasteful drains on present possibilities. *Now* is your great moment.

Similarly, we often find ourselves wishing that we were in some other place. We want to go beyond, to explore, to seek the perfect happiness that we believe lies just over the next hill or beyond the next star. Our own life space seems filled with drudgery and limitations, and we are haunted with the feeling of need to escape into a larger and better world. But *here* is the only place we can act. We can prepare for development and discovery, recognizing that our present condition is not static, but at any moment of our lives, we can act only in the place where we happen to be. *Here* is your great place.

As we gain confidence in our personal strengths, we will be able to more frequently identify opportunities to apply techniques and strategies that fit well into our individual parental styles. Increasingly, we will respond to our children in ways that are helpful, not in ways that simply satisfy needs of our own; and we will begin gradually to see increasing evidence that our efforts are paying off.

A toddler sets aside his jealous feelings about the little one who has invaded his domain and gains satisfaction from carrying the baby's bottle to him and resisting the urge to take a nip. The little guy shows his appreciation for the frustrating hours you spent assembling his tricycle on

Christmas Eve by turning off all the lights except those on the tree, climbing up on your lap, and giving you a peanut-butter-scented kiss. The kindergartner, without being told he must, shares his party treats with his younger brothers. The sisters give up fighting long enough to prepare breakfast in bed for you on Mother's Day.

These are milestones. They mark the progress of our children along Becoming Road. We all have many natural reactions to unlearn. Each word or action of our children that lifts them—even for a moment—above these less noble behaviors is a step forward. Using our natural strengths well is an important means of helping our children become what they were meant to be.

Or perhaps our children will simply be more able to accept the things that happen in their lives. Like the youngster whose grandmother asked him, "Did you get everything you wanted for Christmas?" He replied with deep insight, "No, but that's all right. It's not *my* birthday."

PSYCHOLOGY'S NEW SONG

This book is my attempt to help you enjoy parenthood. I've shared with you some of the happiness I've experienced in fatherhood. I've offered some insights I've gained as a psychologist.

The psychology of proud parenthood sings a new song. Gone from the hit charts is the incriminating lyric that rested too long in the top slot:

> Two things have mixed up your kid
> And hampered his personal growth:
> His genes and environment did,
> And you can take credit for both.

Now we turn up the amplifiers, and, backed by howling infants and jabbering teens, we sing:

Two things that let your child live
Awaken new joy in your soul:
The life and the love that you give
Are making the two of you whole.

The sacrifices seem trivial—like the mornings I pace
from one of our two bathrooms to the other and finally
resign myself to shaving in the car on my way to work. Why,
you ask, only two bathrooms? With two toilets running and
four faucets dripping, who needs more?

Then, of course, there are the money problems. Just
bringing children into the world is tremendously expensive.
Hospitalization costs have gone up so much that many
hospitals now have recovery rooms right next to the
cashier's office. In one hospital they have a sign like the
ones you see in hotel rooms, "Have you left anything?" It
should have said, "Have you anything left?"

As the children get bigger, it costs more and more to
provide for them. This means doing without some other
things. Parents of large families find themselves still
wearing the styles that the fashion experts are trying to
bring back. I remember that when I was very young I
always wanted to wear long pants. Now, thanks to the
precious poverty my family has brought me, no one I know
wears his pants longer than I do. It's fun, though, sending
your clothes to the cleaners and hoping to get somebody
else's back by mistake.

Home furnishings, too, are less than the most modern.
You're likely to find a lot of antiques in two kinds of
homes—those with money and those with children.

But what is all this compared to the marvel of generating
new life? Carl Sandburg looked upon the infant as "God's
opinion that the world should go on."

Step outside some clear night and look up at the stars.

Begin counting the stars you can see, and imagine the millions of heavenly bodies out there that you cannot see. Far more precious than all this magnificence is the person of one single child—any child, black or white, genius or slow learner, whole or deformed.

And I have eight!

How insignificant the sacrifices are compared to the joy that accompanies a son or daughter's first step toward your extended arms! How insignificant the inconveniences compared to the delight of watching young minds growing to reach out toward the new discoveries that come with each new day. See the toddler splashing at the sprinkler on the front lawn, the barefoot youngster sipping his iced drink while the sidewalk scorches his feet, the budding biologist wondering at the why of a worm.

Watch the little one take a tentative lick at a lime lollipop and hand it to you saying, "I'll wait till it gets ripe." Help a young heart to realize that the unattainable pot of gold for which he is crying isn't really worth the tears. Listen to him as he talks of other dreams to be realized. Walk with a child through the gardens of his pleasures, and share the unbounded wealth that comes with seeing the world again through the eyes of youth.

This is joy.

HOW WOULD YOU REACT?

PARENT-CHILD INTERACTION

If you truly want to be proud of your parenthood, it's important that you understand yourself. I emphasized this point in chapter 3 and then built the next five chapters on this principle. The checklist in chapter 3 gave you a chance to identify the kind of person you think you are. I hope it helped you decide which parts of the rest of the book were most important for you.

Sometimes it helps to take a more careful look at ourselves. That's the purpose of this last section of the book. On the pages that follow, you'll find sixty make-believe situations in which a parent responds in three different ways to a child's behavior. We'll call these interaction samples. Thirty of the samples center on interaction between mother and child, and thirty others on father-child interaction.

Basically, these interaction samples are intended to help you understand yourself better, not to test your knowledge of the best methods of child rearing. Try to put yourself and your spouse in the position of the fictitious parents. For each sample involving a parent of your own sex, choose the behavior that comes closest to how you think you *should* react and the one that most nearly shows how you *would* react. For parents of the opposite sex, decide how your spouse should and would respond.

As you use this book to increase your awareness and understanding of yourself, you are applying a measurement technique that psychologists call *self-report*. The accuracy of this composite picture of yourself depends chiefly on three considerations: (1) how accurate your self-perception is; (2) how honest you have been in answering the samples; and (3) how precise the measuring instrument is. As a check on the first two considerations, you might use your spouse's answers to the items he or she applies to you. With regard to the third consideration, I am professionally obliged to emphasize that these interaction samples don't purport to be a scientifically developed personality test.

I have used the first five interaction samples for each sex in speaking to several PTAs. In this way, I have collected information about how other parents think they and their spouses should and would respond. I have data from over three hundred parents. Obviously, this doesn't make the results foolproof, but it's better than mere guesswork.

Each interaction sample begins with the narrative of a situation in which a parent is involved with one or more of the children in the family. The parent is then represented as responding to the situation in three different ways. In reading each sample, first select the parent response alternative that you think represents the way a parent *should* behave.

Next, for the samples involving the parent of your sex,

select the alternative that best represents how you most likely *would* respond to the situation. If the parent in the sample is of the opposite sex, choose the alternative that represents how your spouse would be most likely to respond.

FOR THE FEMALE PARENT

SHOWING OFF

It's Mother's club night, and Sherman Showman, eight, is doing his best to disrupt the sociability of the evening. The latest in his series of antics is standing on his head in the middle of the living room. As he loses his balance and goes down, he kicks one of the club ladies in the ankle, and she registers an expression of pain.

A. "I'm sorry he hurt you, Edna," Mother says, and immediately redirects the conversation to earlier subjects. Meantime, she thinks, "I'll have to spend some time playing with Sherman tomorrow morning."
Sherman gets the candy dish and offers Mrs. Brown a piece, saying, "I'm sorry." Mother responds with, "Passing the candy around is a good idea, Sherman."

B. "Oh, come on now, Edna," Mrs. Showman says. "I'm sure that didn't hurt that much. After all, he's just a child. Sherman sure has a lot of physical agility. I think he'll be a great athlete some day."

C. "That did it!" exclaims Mother. "Sherman, say good-night and get to bed immediately. I thought I'd let you stay up a little while on this special night, but you've shown me you can't behave. Now get yourself up to bed."

STEALING

Yesterday Mrs. Evasive noticed her purse in disorder and five dollars missing. Today she sees her daughter Eva, nine, giving candy to a large group of neighborhood children. A few times before there has been some evidence of petty thievery, but this is the first time Mother has felt sure.

A. "Well, it's only a few dollars," Mother says to herself. "And she doesn't have many friends. Besides, how can I really be sure she stole the money?" Mother goes on with her cleaning and resolves to dismiss the matter from her mind.

B. When Eva comes back to the house, Mother asks, "Where did you get the candy, Eva?"

"What candy?" Eva says.

"I saw you giving candy to all the kids. Where did you get it?"

"The man at the store gave it to me," Eva replies.

"Eva, you know that's not true!" Mother exclaims. "If there's anything I can't stand it's a liar or a thief."

C. "Eva," Mother says calmly to her when she comes back inside, "I saw you giving candy to the kids. I know you took the money from my purse, and I'm disappointed."

Eva looks shocked, but says nothing.

"Next time you need money, come and tell me. We'll talk it over. Just helping yourself is stealing, and that's dishonest. Now you'll have to use your allowance to pay back what you've taken."

TEASING

Ann Annoyance, thirteen, and her sister Joan, nine, are at it again. These squabbles always start the same way, with

Ann wanting something Joan has, and teasing her until Joan gets angry and strikes back. Then a fight follows, which Ann, of course, wins. Thus she takes possession of the desired object.

This time it's the comic book that Joan has been reading. "You can't read that book, Four Eyes," Ann says. "You're too dumb."

A. Mother goes on with her ironing. Very soon the fight breaks out. She lets the whole thing go until Ann has made her conquest and Joan comes crying to her.

"Let her have the book if it means that much to her," Mother says. "It isn't that important, Joan."

B. "That did it!" Mother exclaims. She charges angrily at Ann. "Control that nasty mouth of yours!" she exclaims, shaking her finger in Ann's face.

C. "Ann, come here," Mother says as soon as she hears Ann's comment.

"Why?" Ann says as she comes into the room.

"If you want the book she's looking at that bad, just ask her for it. Or wait till she's finished." Then, setting down the iron, she goes on, "The two of you have to learn to work out compromises."

WHINING

It's time for Winnie Whimper, eleven, to dry dishes. Tonight, unfortunately, her one regular chore conflicts with the time of her favorite TV program.

"I never get to watch what I want on TV," she complains to Mother. "There's always something going on that keeps me from seeing my program. Why can't the old dishes just dry themselves?"

A. "That would be nice, wouldn't it?" Mother agrees. "If only we didn't have things we *had* to do." Then she says more firmly, "But this is the only chore we insist that you do regularly. Now turn off the TV and grab a towel."

B. "Cut out that whining and get out here and do your job!" Mother exclaims. "No matter what I tell you to do, you think I'm picking on you. I said you're going to dry dishes and that's final."

C. "All right," Mother concedes, "if that program is that important to you. I suppose the dishes can dry themselves for one night. I hate to make you give up anything you like that much."

SHYNESS

Sharon Shy, nine, is playing quietly in her room. Mother passes the door and realizes that it has been over two weeks since Sharon last played outside or had friends in. The quietude has been pleasant, but Mother is concerned about the fact that Sharon, who has always been timid, now seems to have no interest in other people.

Stepping into the doorway, she suggests, "Sharon, it's such a pretty day. Why don't you go outside and look up some of the other kids?"

"I don't want to," Sharon says. "They play too rough."

A. Mother replies, "Well, you can't just sit here in the room by yourself all the time. Get out in the kitchen and wash the dishes for me."

"Maybe I can force her outside by making it less pleasant to stay in," Mother thinks.

B. "They do get awfully rough sometimes, don't they, Sharon?" Mother says, coming into the room. "You play very well in games that are more peaceful. I remember some of the games you used to play with Beth. They were fun."

Then Mrs. Shy says to herself, "Maybe next week I can arrange to have some of her friends in."

C. "The only thing to do about shyness is to ignore it," Mother thinks. "Forcing will only make it worse." She shrugs her shoulders and continues through the hall.

RUDENESS

The Rude family is entertaining the Bakers at dinner. In the middle of the conversation, while waiting for dessert, Rudy Rude, thirteen, belches loudly. It is obviously a deliberate belch, an attempt to bring special embarrassment. Mrs. Baker scowls her disapproval.

A. "Well, I'm sure he couldn't help it, Helen," Mrs. Rude says. "After all, he's just a boy. I don't think you have to look so disapprovingly at him."

"Some nerve!" she goes on thinking. "Just look at that Bob Baker sitting there with his elbows on the table."

B. "I'm sorry that happened, Helen," Mother says. "Did you enjoy your weekend in Chicago? How is your sister getting along?"

She then makes a mental note: "Loud belches have to cease. A short dialogue after the Bakers leave is a must. Maybe I can find out why Rudy does things like that."

C. Mother pretends not to hear Rudy's belch. She remembers reading that ignoring misconduct is the best way to deal with it. "Don't give him the satisfaction of knowing he has embarrassed you," she thinks.

She goes on cutting the cake. Mrs. Baker looks puzzled and finally shakes her finger at Rudy, who retaliates by sticking his tongue out at her.

VULGARITY

Cass Custer, ten, has been playing with her little sister in their room. All is apparently calm when suddenly a burst of profanity, uttered without apparent emotion, issues from Cass's lips.

Mother, just outside the room, stops short as she hears this. Cass has used strong language before, but nothing like this! And it's always been when she was angry.

A. Mother steps into the room and looks disapprovingly at Cass. Immediately aware of her presence, Cass looks up.

"I don't think that's very nice language for you to use, Cass," she says. After a brief pause she continues: "What in the world happened to bring that on?"

B. Mother moves quickly into the room. "I don't know where she hears that kind of language," she thinks. "She sure doesn't hear me talking like that." Inside the door, she says to Cass, "I heard that, young lady. I don't want you playing with those Myer kids any more. They pick up all that dirty talk from their mother."

C. "What did you say?" Mother fumes as she storms into the room. "Never in all my life have I heard a child talk like that. Wait till I tell your father. He'll give you a good beating."

LYING

The story Freddie Fraud told his mother was a master-piece of seven-year-old inventiveness. It came complete with a six-foot-tall tiger that had escaped from the zoo and chased him up the street. But it was really a lot more narrative than might have been required to expain the hole in the back of his new trousers.

As Mother looks at him in disbelief, Freddie's large brown eyes look squarely into hers, and he says, "Honest, Mom!"

A. "OK," Mother says, "if you say so, that's good enough for me."

"No use pressuring him on this storytelling bit," she thinks. "He'll grow out of it. Some day he might make a fortune writing best sellers."

B. "That's the most ridiculous story I've ever heard!" Mother says angrily. "I've told you before I don't want you lying to me! Now, I want you to tell me how you really tore your pants. And I want the truth!"

C.   Mother smiles, walks over to Freddie, and puts her arm around his shoulder. "That's a great story, dear," she says. "But you know it didn't really happen. It's a shame that you tore your nice new pants, but Mother can fix them up so they look almost new again."

CHEATING

Mrs. Cheatham has just read a note from teacher about her son Chester, thirteen. The note advises her that Chester has recently turned in several papers that are exact duplicates of those submitted by his friend Carmen Carbon.

"How does this happen?" Mother asks Chester.

He replies, "Carmen is my friend, and he gets mad if I don't let him copy my work."

A. "But that's dishonest!" Mother says. Chester looks ashamed. Then Mrs. Cheatham continues: "But I can see it would be difficult for you to say no to Carmen. It *is* important for you to keep your friends. But don't you think you'd better tell him to change some of the answers so it won't be so obvious he's copied from you?"

B. "But Chester," Mother says, "that's dishonest. And besides, you're not really helping your friend by letting him copy from you." Then, seeing his shamefaced expression, she adds, "I know it's difficult, but you're going to have to say no to him next time. If he really wants to be your friend, this won't really change anything."

C. "Let him get mad!" Mother says excitedly. "What kind of friend is it that gets you into trouble all the time?" She feels the emotion swelling inside. "You tell that kid that he's not going to copy from you any more!"

ANGER

"Shit!" says eleven-year-old Ira Irascible. It's half under his breath, but Mother is almost sure that's what she hears. And she's even surer that Ira is as angry as she's ever seen him. His facial muscles are tight, and the vein at his left temple stands out. Mother doesn't know what happened while he was playing with his little sister to cause his obvious anger.

A. Calmly, Mother leads Ira out of the room. Once beyond Sis's earshot, she says, "She gets you mad sometimes, doesn't she?"

"I hate her," Ira says, just loud enough to be sure his sister gets the message.

Mother looks back at Sis, standing the doorway. Mrs. Irascible motions for her daughter to come, puts an arm around each child, and says, "Anytime people spend a lot of time together, they're bound to get very angry at each other once in a while. Let's talk about what happened."

B. Mother goes on with her ironing. "No use making a big deal out of a small incident," she thinks. "He's only using language he hears from his father."

C. Quickly, Mother sets the iron down. Calming herself, she goes over to where Ira is sitting. "What did you say, Ira?"

"Nothing," he responds.

"Well, I heard it. Listen, young man, we won't have you losing your temper and using bad language around here. If you can't play nicely, you can spend the rest of the afternoon in your room."

FIGHTING

Tom Tuff, nine, has been playing with his brother Tony, seven, just outside the kitchen window. Passing by, Mother notices some kind of disagreement between the two boys. She pauses to watch.

Tony has the whiffle ball they've been playing with and is backing away with arm cocked, ready to throw it to Tom. Suddenly Tom lunges at him and pokes him hard in the stomach. "I said I want the ball!" Tom yells.

A. Through the open window Mother says, "There you are fighting again. The neighbors must think that's all you ever do. Well, that's only because you learned it from those Thompson kids. Now come inside before somebody gets hurt."

B. "Come in here right now, Tom!" Mother yells through the window.

As he comes, with obvious unwillingness, into the house, Mother hits him with the flat of her hand. "That's to show you how it feels," she says angrily. "We don't stand for that hitting stuff around here."

C. "OK, it's time to come in, boys," Mrs. Tuff says. Reluctantly, Tom and Tony comply. As they enter the kitchen, Mother continues, "Tony, I want you to run up to the store for me. And, Tom, I need your help with a couple of jobs." Then she thinks, "I've got to talk to Tom about his bullying."

CRYING

Betty Bawler, ten, has always been a very sensitive child who cries easily. Today, she fell off her bicycle, and she has come into the house crying, with scuffed elbow and knee. Mother is in the kitchen and sees her as soon as she comes in.

A. "What happened, dear?" Mother asks.
"I fell off my bike!" Betty wails. "Skinned my elbow and knee."
"Come here; let me see." With arm around Betty, Mother examines the skinned areas. Then, "Go in and wash it off. Maybe you'd better put a bandage on that elbow."

B. "All right, what happened this time?" Mother asks.
"I fell off my bike!" Betty wails.
"Well, don't yell like you're half-killed. Why take it out on me? I can't help it that you can't ride. I suppose you'll say that's my fault, too."

C. Mother goes on with her work. "I can't afford to encourage her crying all the time by paying attention to her." she thinks.

Then, glancing up, she sees the blood oozing from Betty's elbow. "Go in the bathroom and wash it off and put a bandage on it," Mother says.

SULKING

Ten-year-old Simon Sullen is pouting in his room. He asked to go out and play, but it is raining and he already has a cold. Mother's refusal caused him to express his disapproval and walk off angrily.

A. Mother tries to go on with her work and suppress the anger she feels surging inside. "But I can't let him go on sulking like that," she says to herself. "He's got to get over it."

Finally, she walks up to Simon's room, throws open the door, and calls him to her. "You've got to stop this sulking around," she says, administering a forceful swat to his backside.

B. "He'll get over it," she thinks. "I'll have to let him sulk now, but next time I have to say no I'll at least try to let him know I understand his feelings."

C. "I can't stand that sulking," Mother thinks. "If he gets a worse cold, it'll serve him right."

"All right!" she calls upstairs. "You can go out and catch pneumonia for all I care."

SOLITUDE

For the third time today, the neighborhood friends of Sophie Solitaire, eleven, are calling outside. Once again, Sophie is on her way to tell them she doesn't want to come out to play. Sophie has only a few friends, and Mother recognizes that she will soon lose them if she doesn't show some interest in them.

A. "Sophie," she says firmly, "I'm not telling you again. Get out there and play. I'm tired of having you mope around the house. How on earth do you ever expect to have any friends?"

B. Mrs. Solitaire says, "Your friends sure seem to enjoy playing with you." Sophie's frown is unchanged. "You don't feel much like playing outside today, do you?" Mother continues. "I guess there are just some days when we all feel more like being alone. Why don't you tell your friends you'll call them tomorrow, and you can play together then?"

C. "Sophie, I told you before, " Mother says, "I want you to go out and play."

"I don't feel like playing outside."

"But you're moping around the house far too much these days," Mother replies. "You need to get out and play with your friends if you hope to keep them."

Sophie begins to cry. "I don't care if I don't have any friends," she says. "I don't like those girls anyway."

"Well, all right, if that's the way you feel about it," Mother says. "But don't blame me if you find you don't have anybody to play with."

INFERIORITY

A couple of the older girls that Cora Coward, six, plays with want to help her learn to ride her bike. Cora comes crying to Mother, protesting that she doesn't feel good. This is her standard excuse whenever she feels she needs to avoid a difficult situation.

A. "It upsets you when you're not sure about something, doesn't it?" Mother says. "And this sort of makes you feel bad. That's all right. There are a lot of things you do very well. Sometime when you feel ready, you can go out and try to get used to the bike gradually. You can probably learn all by yourself."

B. "Get outside!" Mother shouts. "I'm sick and tired of hearing about your phony aches and pains!"

C. "OK, Cora, you may stay in and play. I'll tell the girls you have a bad cold. Riding a bike isn't so important. Besides, you'll be a lot safer inside the way some of the kids around here hot-rod up and down the street."

FOR THE MALE PARENT

SHOWING OFF

Eighteen-year-old Shelley Showman is entertaining her boyfriend in the living room while Dad is trying to figure out his income tax. Mr. Showman is only vaguely aware that Shirley, age six, has also gone into the living room.

"Dad!" Shelley suddenly exclaims. "Make Shirley get out of here. She's showing off again."

A. "That's your problem," Dad retorts. "Stop bothering me with your stupid fighting. I've got to get this tax figured out."

B. "Shirley!" Dad yells furiously, "get up to your room and stay there. I've told you a hundred times to stop that showing off all the time."

C. "Shirley," Dad says calmly, "come here a minute. I need your help." When Shirley comes into the room he requests, "Would you take these two pencils in and sharpen them for me?"

Then he thinks, "I've got to try to find out what's behind her constant need for attention."

STEALING

Eleven-year-old Everett Evasive and his father have just finished hitting golf balls at the driving range and are on their way back to the car.

"Hey, Dad, look!" Everett says. From each pocket he takes two golf balls. All four balls are clearly marked with the red stripe of the driving range.

A. "What the hell do you think this is?" Mr. Evasive exclaims, "Do you want to get arrested for stealing golf balls? You kids today have no respect for other people's property. Now take those balls and turn them in at the equipment stand!"

B. "Hey, I guess we'd better take those balls over and turn them in," Mr. Evasive says, "We only paid to hit them, not to keep them."

"Aw, they'll never miss four balls," Everett complains.

"If everybody that comes here walked off with four, I guess they'd soon miss them," Dad says. "The balls aren't ours. We have no right to them." He puts his arm over Everett's shoulder and guides him toward the equipment stand.

C. A little surprised at first, Mr. Evasive tries not to let it show. "I guess you can use those to practice putting in the backyard," he says to Everett.

Opening the car door, he thinks, "Why make a major production out of this whole thing? It's only four balls. Everybody probably walks off with a few."

TEASING

Andy Annoyance, thirteen, has an unusually large repertoire of nasty names for his younger brother, Amos. This weekend he has hit on one that strikes a particularly sensitive chord.

Mr. Annoyance is watching the Sunday afternoon football game when he hears Andy's chant: "Ignor-amos, Ignor-amos, Ignor-amos!" He sees Amos take a swing at his older brother, but Andy's ability to dodge is as effective as his vocabulary. Andy laughs, and Amos breaks into tears.

A. "Cut the name-calling and fighting, guys." Mr. Annoyance says. "Come in here and watch this replay." As they enter the room and sit on either side of him, Dad gives Amos a comforting pat on the back. "Watch this fantastic interception," he says to both boys.

B. Dad resists his impulse to correct Andy for name-calling. "Andy," he says laughing, "lately you sure do come up with some dillies!" Then he leans forward to watch the instant replay while the boys continue to go at it.

C. "Knock that stuff off!" Mr. Annoyance exclaims, "All you kids ever do is fight. Get outside with your noise so I can watch this game."

WHINING

Just this evening, Mrs. Whimper expressed concern to her husband that their son, Wallace, nine, seemed to be becoming a hypochondriac. Now as Mr. Whimper is trying to read the evening paper, Wallace is lying on the couch making strange noises. Finally Mother says, "What seems to be the trouble, Wally?"

"My leg hurts," Wallace moans. Mrs. Whimper gives her husband a "see-what-I-mean" look.

A. "Hmm," Dad hums sympathetically, "you've had one heck of a long day. When we're tired everything seems to hurt just that much more."

B. "Here, I'll help you up to bed," Dad offers. "If that pain keeps up, we'll have to take you to the doctor and have him take a look at your leg."

C. "So what are you looking at me for?" Mr. Whimper says to his wife. "You're the one that's always babying the kid." Then to Wallace he says, "Now you stop whining and get up to bed."

SHYNESS

Mrs. Shy is laid up with the flu, and her husband has to get the weekly groceries in. He takes Seymour, six, along to the market with him to keep him out of his mother's hair.

It seems that every time this happens, they've rearranged all the things in the store. "Ask the man where the napkins are," Mr. Shy instructs Seymour, pointing to the clerk.

Seymour frowns, pops his thumb into his mouth, and turns away.

A. Father reaches down, jerks Seymour's hand away from his face, and smacks his rear end.

"I should have known better than to bring you along," he says. "Next time you can stay home. I'll find the napkins myself."

B. Paying no attention to Seymour, Father walks over to check with the clerk. "There's no use pressuring him," he thinks. "To force him will only make things worse. He'll just have to grow out of his backwardness."

C. "Let's see whether we can find out where those napkins are," Father says, leaning slightly toward Seymour while starting to push the cart toward the clerk. "I'll bet if this man will just give us a clue, you'll be able to find them right away. Remember how you found the book we'd looked all over the house for? That was great."

RUDENESS

Mr. Rude is following his family into church when ten-year-old Ruby darts in front of old Mrs. Schaeffer and nearly knocks her down. With no sign of being aware of Mrs. Schaeffer, Ruby looks back at her brother and sticks her tongue out at him. The old woman gasps.

A. "I'm sorry, Mrs. Schaeffer," Dad says. "Ruby, slow down and hold the door for Mrs. Schaeffer. Sometimes we get so busy with our own concerns that we forget about others."

Then he says to himself, "If we could just instill a little more self-confidence in her, maybe Ruby wouldn't have to be so self-centered."

B. Dad returns Mrs. Schaeffer's cold stare, "After all," he thinks, "she was just playing. Kids are like that." He reaches out to hold the door for Mrs. Schaeffer.

C. "Ruby!" Dad exclaims, "Be careful! You almost knocked Mrs. Schaeffer down. She must think we never teach you any manners or consideration for other people."

VULGARITY

Calvin Custer, eight, has been expanding his vocabulary. A few of the new words he uses are in his speller. More often, he astounds Mr. and Mrs. Custer with the kind of expression that gets bleeped out on TV.

Today he is coming out of the bathroom when he bumps his elbow on the door frame. Profane polysyllables fly freely. Dad is right there to take care of the situation.

A. Without a word, Dad gives Calvin a solid blast to the backside. "Where the—bleep—did you learn—bleep—words like that?" he yells. "We don't talk like that around here! Now go back in there and wash your dirty mouth out with soap!"

B. "Ouch," Mr. Custer says. "That hurt, I guess, didn't it?" But I don't like to think you have to use language like that to express your hurt."

Watching Calvin's reaction, Dad thinks, "Enough said. He probably uses some of that language to impress me. We won't make too much of it."

C. "Don't you think it's time to get busy with your homework?" Dad suggests. He tells himself, "All the kids talk that way now. We parents can't do anything about what they learn at school."

LYING

It's a Saturday afternoon when Mr. Fraud finds the light fixture in ten-year-old Fanny's room broken. It was working last night, and no one except Fanny has been in the room since.

Dad calls for Fanny to come. She registers surprise when she sees the light fixture. "How did that happen?" she asks convincingly.

A. Dad feels his anger rise rapidly. "You know very well how it happened!" he shouts. "You're always messing around and throwing things in here. Then you try to act like you don't know anything about it. I can't stand dishonesty!"

B. "You mean you don't know anything about it?" Dad asks. Even though he feels sure Fanny is responsible, he doesn't want to accuse her. "OK, then," he goes on, "I'll fix it this afternoon."

C. "Fanny," Dad says, "I can't believe that you don't know anything about this. Now be truthful and tell me what happened. It's only a light fixture, and it's much more important that you accept responsibility for your actions."

CHEATING

Charmaine Cheatham, fourteen, is preparing for a test. She has a small roll of calculator tape half-full of notes when Dad comes into the room. As Charmaine scrambles to hide the tape, Mr. Cheatham remembers hearing two boys at the church social joking about an eighth-grade girl who hid crib notes in her bra.

A. "Let's see what you have on the tape," Dad says.

"Just some school notes," Charmaine says, unwinding a few inches of the tape. "This helps me study better. Like putting it all into a computer."

"Written notes do help," Mr. Cheatham says. "The important thing is to get as much knowledge as possible into your brain. Kids who cheat are being dishonest and are just cheating themselves."

B. "Oh, no!" says Mr. Cheatham, shocked at Charmaine's dishonesty. But then the whole thing suddenly seems very funny. His own daughter!

As Charmaine eyes him with wonder and embarrassment, Dad says, "That's really clever! I think every kid cheats sometimes, but you have a great system."

C. "Give me that tape!" Mr. Cheatham shouts. "I sure didn't think I'd ever catch you cheating!" He hurls the tape across the room. "And I'd better not ever catch you again!"

ANGER

Ida Irascible, eleven, is being scolded by her mother for not doing her chores. Dad is just thinking that Mother's handling of the situation is unusually expert when he hears Ida shout, "Aw, shut up!" Ida says something else in an angry tone and slams the door to the basement.

A. Jumping up from his chair, Dad storms into the kitchen. He grabs Ida by the arm and says firmly, "I heard that, Ida. You're not going to talk that way to your mother and get away with it. We're grounding you for two weeks: no going out, no television, no telephone. Behavior like that we just can't tolerate."

B. Dad waits a moment to see what Mother's response will be. Mrs. Irascible orders, "Go tell your father what you just said."

As Ida comes slowly into the room, Mr. Irascible confronts her with a stern look. "It's Peggy's turn to mop," Ida says.

"That could be," Dad says. "We'll check to make sure you're both doing your fair share. But you'll have to work at showing respect for your parents. Now you think about what you want to say to your mother, and I'll ask Mom about Peggy."

C. Dad goes on reading the paper. When Mother tells Ida to go in to him, he tries not to listen.

"Your mother's going to have to handle her own problems," he says. "Sometimes the more attention you pay to this kind of thing, the worse it gets."

FIGHTING

Tanya Tuff, twelve, is fighting with her sister Tammy, who is two years older. The disagreement is over a scarf, which each girl maintains belongs to her. As Mr. Tuff works on a faucet repair job, he hears the two girls arguing vociferously.

Suddenly there is a ripping sound, and Dad guesses that the girls have torn the scarf in their struggle. The sound of hand striking skin is heard next, and Tanya comes crying into the kitchen.

"You dirty rat!" she yells. Then, "Daddy, Tammy hit me and tore my scarf!"

"It was my scarf!" Tammy shouts from the other room.

A. Dad lays down his wrench and calls Tammy into the kitchen. When she enters, he says to both girls, "You're not going to get me into the middle of your fights. I don't know whose scarf it was, but I'm sure you can work out a peaceful solution to the problem. Let's talk about what just happened."

B. "I don't give a damn whose scarf it was!" Father says angrily. "You're going to stop that fighting all the time. How can a man get anything done around this place? Now both of you get out of here, or I'm going to give you a good beating."

C. "Don't try to get me involved in your fights," Dad says. "You women are all alike. Every time you see something somebody else has, you fight like wildcats to get it. Just leave me out of it."

CRYING

Billy Bawler, nine, nearly always brings his homework to his father for checking. Tonight is no exception. As Mr. Bawler looks down the page of math problems, he spots three mistakes. Billy seems sad when Father points out the first mistake, sniffles on the second, and with the third, bursts into tears.

A. "Well, you asked me to check it," Father reminds him. "It's not my fault that you make dumb mistakes. I know I've gone over this stuff with you a hundred times. Instead of crying, why don't you pay attention and learn for a change?"

B. Mr. Bawler grits his teeth, determined not to show his anger. "Nothing gets me madder," he thinks, "than for a nine-year-old to cry like a baby." He says nothing about the tears, but simply hands the paper back to his son, thinking, "We'll just keep ignoring this. Sooner or later, he'll grow out of it."

C. "Don't worry about it, Bill," says Mr. Bawler. "We all make mistakes. And it hurts when we've tried hard and then someone tells us we're wrong." He puts his hand on his son's shoulder. "Give those three problems one more try—OK?"

SULKING

Sibyl Sullen, nine, is sulking in the living room when Dad comes home from work. "What's the trouble, Sugar?" Dad inquires.

Sibyl is silent for a few moments and then says, "Mom won't let me go to Ginny's party tonight."

A. "That's a shame," Dad agrees. "I guess you were kind of counting on it, weren't you?"

"Aw, can't I go, Dad?" Sibyl implores. "All the kids will be there."

Dad looks at her sympathetically and then says, "It's always tough to miss out on something important. Let me find out why Mom thinks you shouldn't go."

B. "Why not?" Dad asks.

Sibyl shrugs and then says, "I don't know. You know how Mom gets sometimes. You just can't talk to her."

Dad responds, "Oh, I can handle Mom all right. You just count on going and I'll work it out with her."

C. "Why not?" Dad asks. And then, without letting Sibyl reply, he says, "What did you do this time? You're always getting yourself into trouble, and then you sulk around forever. Just keep it up and you'll be grounded for a month!"

SOLITUDE

Sam Solitaire, age eleven, is complaining to his father that his younger brother Sol, age ten, refuses to play with him. "He never wants to do anything I want to do," Sam says. "All he ever does is sit in his room and read."

Dad forces himself to put down the newspaper and walk to the door of Sol's room. As he steps into the room, Sol looks up and says, "Why can't I just sit in here by myself?"

A. Dad replies, "I think you should spend some time playing with Sam."

"I don't want to," Sol comes back. "Now leave me alone." Dad hesitates for a moment and then walks away. "I guess he has a right to decide how he spends his time," he thinks.

B. "Put that book away and come on out of there!" Dad says sharply. "What kind of a queer kid are you with your nose buried in a book all the time?"

C. "I think it's great that you enjoy reading so much," Dad says. "And I really like your taste in reading materials." Sol looks surprised. Dad goes on, "Why don't you and Sam figure out some plans for something you'd like to do tomorrow?"

INFERIORITY

The Coward family is at the swimming pool, and everybody is having fun except eight-year-old Caleb. "There's just no way I'll ever learn to swim," he says dejectedly to his mother.

Overhearing the comment, Mr. Coward comes over to the side of the pool.

A. "You can learn the same as everybody else does," he says, trying to encourage Caleb. "Come on in and I'll help you."

Caleb is not persuaded. He moves around behind his mother. Mr. Coward looks at his wife, shrugs, and swims away. "I guess it isn't really important enough to worry about," he thinks.

B. "It takes time," Mr. Coward says. "And it takes a lot of patience. I guess it gets discouraging; you're good at so many other sports, right?"

Caleb nods. Dad holds out his arms to invite Caleb into the pool. Caleb hesitates and then turns away.

"When you get your courage up, come on in," Mr. Coward says. "You'll get on to it, just like baseball."

C. Dad climbs out of the pool and sneaks around behind Caleb. He grabs him, picks him up, and throws him into the water.

"How do you expect to learn how to swim if you don't go into the water!"

Now let's look at your answers. First focus on those samples in which your *would* response is the same as your *should*. These are the strengths that will form the foundation of your effort to be a better parent. Then compare your *should* and *would* answers with the following key. The key shows one man's informed opinion of which response would usually be *most helpful*. Trouble is, when you listen to too much advice, you find yourself making other people's mistakes. Certainly no psychologist can guarantee that any of these responses would or would not be right in your particular family at a particular time.

At any rate, here are the answers *this* psychologist had in mind. For the five interaction samples I used with PTAs, the key shows the percentage choosing the "preferred" (most helpful) answers as would responses. How do you compare?

	Female Parent	Male Parent
Showing Off	A (13%)	C (42%)
Stealing	C (63%)	B (67%)
Teasing	C (44%)	A (28%)
Whining	A (49%)	A (27%)
Shyness	B (56%)	C (45%)
Rudeness	B	A
Vulgarity	A	B
Lying	C	C
Cheating	B	A
Anger	A	B
Fighting	C	A
Crying	A	C
Sulking	B	A
Solitude	B	C
Inferiority	A	B

Did you find that both your *should* and *would* responses
agreed with the "most helpful" alternative in some of the
samples? These samples give you a means of identifying
some of your chief strengths as a parent. You are now ready
to partially answer the question: "What do I do *right* with
my kids?"

Refreshing, isn't it?

Against this backdrop of some of your strong points, we
can now consider your responses as to how you and your
spouse would *probably* react. If you can persuade your
spouse to respond to the samples, it might be helpful to
compare your mutual impressions—without rancor.

Let's consider the responses in groups that correspond to
the kinds of behavior discussed in chapters 4 through 8.

PUNITIVE RESPONSES

	Female Parent	Male Parent
Showing Off	C	B
Shyness	A	A
Vulgarity	C	A
Anger	C	A
Fighting	B	B
Sulking	A	C

ANGRY RESPONSES

	Female Parent	Male Parent
Stealing	B	A
Teasing	B	C
Lying	B	A
Cheating	C	C
Solitude	A	B
Inferiority	B	C

DEFENSIVE RESPONSES

	Female Parent	Male Parent
Showing Off	B	A
Whining	B	C
Rudeness	A	C
Vulgarity	B	C
Fighting	A	C
Crying	B	A

YIELDING RESPONSES

	Female Parent	Male Parent
Teasing	A	B
Whining	C	B
Cheating	A	B
Sulking	C	B
Solitude	C	A
Inferiority	C	A

UNCONCERNED RESPONSES

	Female Parent	Male Parent
Stealing	A	C
Shyness	C	B
Rudeness	C	B
Lying	A	B
Anger	B	C
Crying	C	B

If you find several of your *probable* responses in one of the above groupings, you may want to go back now and review. Chapter 4 discusses punitive responses; 5, angry responses;

6, defensive responses; 7, yielding responses; and 8, unconcerned responses.

Whether you review or not, please keep three things in mind:

1. The traits suggested by your response patterns can be strong points or weak points, depending on how you use them.
2. The choice of what reactions, if any, you try to change is entirely your decision.
3. There's a good chance that your real reactions would be more constructive than those you chose as *would* responses, since you were asked to compare—almost contrast—how you should and would behave.